Leckie ✕ Leckie
Scotland's leading educational publishers

# INTERMEDIATE 2 & HIGHER

# Religious, Moral & Philosophical Studies

## grade **booster**

## ✕ David Jack ✕

# CONTENTS

# 1 Basic stuff

*How will this book help me?*

*How is the book organised?*

*How should I use this book?*

*Before you start*

*The exam structure*

## HOW WILL THIS BOOK HELP ME?

This book is designed to help you get the best possible grade you can manage at Higher or Intermediate 2 Religious, Moral and Philosophical Studies (RMPS from now on because I have no intention of writing that mouthful out every time I mention the exam!).

Don't make the mistake, as some people do, of thinking that RMPS is an easy Higher. Many pupils get good marks in RMPS because they are in S6 and have a stack of Highers already or the person teaching them is just the business or because many pupils put in that extra effort because it takes a bit of guts to do this Higher in the first place. Anybody who decides that they can wing it through this exam with the minimum of effort is going to be really disappointed when the envelope comes through the door in August.

## HOW IS THE BOOK ORGANISED?

This book is part of the Grade Booster Series and its aim is to help people like you get a better grade. The best way to get a better grade is to tackle bits of the course that cause problems for most candidates. *The part of the course that causes the most problems for candidates is the analysis and evaluation*. All those brilliant ideas and contributions you make in class seem to disappear from your cranium the minute you are asked to put pen to paper. So, for that reason, the book is going to give you only brief advice on KU questions, and spend most of its time helping you with AE questions, which are the hardest ones in the whole exam. The following list shows how I have set things out.

- Every topic in paper 1 has been covered and Christianity and Buddhism from paper 2 have been covered.
- Chapter 2 is on exam tactics. It gives you some advice on how to answer KU questions, and some advice that applies to all KU and AE questions.
- Chapter 3 gives examples from each unit of what good answers are and how to build up a good AE answer.
- The remaining chapters pick out the most obvious AE areas for each topic in each unit. It's not possible to cover them all, so it might well be that some areas come up that are not in this book; in which case ... sorry!
- In these chapters there are also examples of the kinds of statements that might precede an AE question or more direct AE questions – this will help you to get used to the wording and get over your fears of these statements, many of which are not nearly as complicated or sophisticated as they look.

## HOW SHOULD I USE THIS BOOK?

There are a few ways you can use this book:

- You can leave it open on your desk to pretend that you really have been studying and not playing your Xbox 360 or sticking scraps in your scrapbook. Be sure to highlight lines in the book and dog-ear the page corners though.
- You can produce it in your RMPS class and tell the teacher that you would recommend this excellent book for the entire class.
- You can dip in and out of it according to the problems you are encountering in your answering techniques, and then apply the suggestions to the next past paper or homework task you do.

## BEFORE YOU START

You need two things before you start to read this book and both are on the SQA website:

- a copy of the SQA Arrangements for the units and options you're doing
- a copy of the Specimen Question Papers.

You may need to refer to these as we go along.

# THE EXAM STRUCTURE

**Intermediate 2:** One paper lasting two hours (four *Simpsons* episodes). You have to answer all the questions in the three sections you have studied.

**Higher:** Two papers. Paper 1 covers Morality in the Modern World and Science and Belief. Paper 2 covers World Religions.

Paper 1 lasts for 1 hour 45 minutes. Then, you have a short tea-break and team-talk from your teacher before launching into the 55 minute Paper 2. After Paper 2 you leave the school and head for the nearest Casualty Department, who will use specialist equipment to get your hand out of the 'pen grasp' in which it has become locked.

Be warned, folks, Higher RMPS is a pretty gruelling exam. It's fifteen minutes shy of three hours, and that is a lot of writing and thinking. You really do need to be on top of your studying, and on top of your game, to do well in this exam.

# 2 Exam tactics

*Tackling the questions*

*General advice on Knowledge and Understanding (KU) questions*

*Things to you need to know, avoid and look out for in KU questions*

*General advice on Analysis and Evaluation (AE) questions*

*Things to you need to know, avoid and look out for in World Religions AE Questions*

*The all-encompassing question: World Religions*

*A few things to remember*

*In case of emergency*

*And finally...*

## TACKLING THE QUESTIONS

KU questions should be pretty straightforward for you. They are about regurgitating facts. They are usually uncomplicated questions and you can make a big killing in terms of marks. AE questions are the ones where most people struggle – they are the big value questions, so scoring high in them is vital.

Let's start by giving you some general advice on KU and AE questions.

## GENERAL ADVICE ON KNOWLEDGE AND UNDERSTANDING (KU) QUESTIONS

Questions looking for KU often have the following words or phrases. They are listed below along with a definition of what the SQA wants from you:

1. *What* or *what* is or *what are* ... straightforward definition or description.
2. *Describe* ... er, describe something.

3. *Give a description* … er, as above, describe something.

4. *In what ways* … describe more than one thing because it says '*ways*'.

# THINGS TO YOU NEED TO KNOW, AVOID AND LOOK OUT FOR IN KU QUESTIONS

Before we start, there are some things that you should do in KU questions. I could have put these things in for every KU question, but teenagers tend not to respond to nagging and end up just getting angry. So, to avoid that, you are being told once. Here goes:

In KU questions you need to **know**:

- examples from real life
- different religious views on issues
- scripture references.

In KU questions you must **avoid**:

- giving personal opinions
- saying that all religious people believe the same
- giving one-word answers.

In KU questions you must be on the **lookout for**:

- chances to quote from scripture or individual believers – quotes get you marks
- times when the English word for the concept is used
- questions that ask you to explain something in a quote from scripture (Int 2 only)
- questions that ask for a particular religious view on an issue

# GENERAL ADVICE ON ANALYSIS AND EVALUATION (AE) QUESTIONS

AE question wording is difficult to predict – these questions can cause the most difficulty because candidates may not understand them. They often have quotes, which is why they are so difficult to predict. (To be honest it is a bad idea to try to predict what will come up because you could be wrong.) Nevertheless, the kinds of AE questions that can be asked are limited in all sections of the paper. The wordings will vary so, as with KU, the trick is to work out which kind of question is being asked on each of the areas. There are some things, though, that **are** quite predictable in AE questions.

Questions looking for AE often have the following words or phrases. They are listed below along with a definition of what the SQA wants from you:

| Question stem | Meaning |
|---|---|
| *Explain, give an explanation...* | Give a reason as to why something is the way it is or why someone has a particular view. |
| *Why...* | Give reasons for something, explain something. |
| *Evaluate...* | Weigh up the good and the bad points about an issue. |
| *To what extent, how far* | Weigh up the good and the bad points about an issue. |
| *How can this be justified?* | Weigh up the good and the bad points about an issue. |
| *Is this a fair comment?* | Weigh up the good and the bad points about an issue. |
| *What are the main drawbacks /benefits/ strengths/weaknesses...* | Pick out the main flaws and strengths of an argument or position. |
| *Do you agree?* | This question is not looking for your opinion at all. It's actually looking for you to give a balanced view of two or more sides of an argument, so **don't make the answer too personal**. |
| *Compare and contrast...* | Give similarities and differences between two or more positions. |
| *How might it be argued...* | Explain the arguments for or against an issue, depending on what the question says. |
| *How effective...* | Weigh up the good and the bad points about an issue. |
| *What is ... the problem with/the issue with ...* | Give a reason why something is the way it is or why someone has a particular view. |
| *How is ... similar to ...* | Give similarities and differences between two or more positions. |
| *Discuss ...* | Give a balanced view of two or more sides of an argument. |
| *Comment ...* | Give a balanced view of two or more sides of an argument. |

When there is a statement in an AE question, it is usually followed by questions **such as the ones below**.

You should bear these questions in mind when you are looking at the grids later on. In fact, rip this page out and have it lying alongside each set of questions as you get to them. That way, you'll not wear out the pages flicking back and forward, and the school will have to buy a new set of books which will pay for my long overdue cosmetic surgery.

- How might religious people respond to this statement?
- To what extent is this true?
- How far do you agree?
- Why might religious people agree with this statement?
- Explain why some religious people would disagree with this statement.
- How might some religious people support this view?
- Why might some religious people criticise this view?
- Explain how this statement might be defended by religious people.
- Explain how one secular view you have studied would respond to this statement.
- To what extent is this true?
- How far do you agree?
- Why might there be agreement with this statement?
- Explain why some religious people would disagree with this statement.
- Why might some people support this view?
- Why might some people criticise this view?
- Explain how this statement might be defended by religious people.
- Explain a secular response to this statement.
- Why might this be considered a weakness of religious arguments against whatever?
- Explain the evidence that could be used to support this secular argument as a strength of the whatever.
- How justified is this claim?
- In relation to whatever, explain the responses religious people might have to this statement.

There are many more possibilities and combinations. In fact, next time you have an empty and invite your friends round, a good icebreaker is to have them make up RMPS questions.

# THINGS YOU NEED TO KNOW, AVOID AND LOOK OUT FOR IN WORLD RELIGIONS AE QUESTIONS

As with the KU questions, there are some things that you should do in AE questions. Here goes.

In AE questions you need to **know**:

- scriptural references
- at least two views of what you are studying.

In AE questions you must **avoid**:

- going off on some kind of personal rant that has nothing to do with the question
- making statements about issues without supporting them with examples, quotes or further details
- writing everything you know about the topic without referring to the question
- repeating information that you have already used in the paper, because that could cost you time and marks
- making outrageous statements about the religion – keep the middle line.

In AE questions you must **look out for**:

- any chance to use scriptures, quotes or examples from real life – they get marks!

# THE ALL-ENCOMPASSING QUESTION: WORLD RELIGIONS

There is one area of questioning that has yet to be explored – AE questions that cross over each of the organising principles of the course. That is, there can be questions with combinations of the goals or the means or the human condition. The ways in which this can be questioned are too numerous to list fully, but the most common ones are noted below:

- how the means to the goals help overcome the problems of the human condition
- how the means to the goals help achieve the goals of life
- which of the means to the goals is the most helpful in achieving the goals of life/overcoming the problems of the human condition

- how certain concepts in the goals, means and human condition are linked together
- how certain concepts in the goals, means and human condition may contradict or support each other
- whether the goals of life can be achieved by only one of the means
- whether the human condition can be understood by only one of the means
- why the religion might be considered negative through its teachings on the human condition, goals and means
- why the religion might be considered to give hope through its teaching on the human condition, goals and means
- the extent to which the religion gives a good assessment of the human condition and how to overcome it.

# A FEW THINGS TO REMEMBER

Before we finish with this, there is some other basic stuff that you really ought to know. Some of it might be screamingly obvious to you, but to some others it is not. Even the most sensible of pupils can do crazy things in the Int 2 and Higher RMPS exams.

## A few must dos

- You must check what sections you are doing and perhaps have them tattooed on some part of your body that you can see.
- You must attempt to answer **all** the questions in the sections you have to do. If you miss a question out then you are certain to get zero, zilch, nada, nowt. If you make an attempt at the question then, you never know, you have nothing to lose.
- If you do not know what a question is about, go on and do other questions. Don't just sit there biting your lip. If at the end of this you still do not know what it is about and no words ring a bell at all, write about something that has not turned up in other questions – again, you never know, and markers have to read everything you write.
- Make sure you know a few quotes, or individuals or organisations that have said something about the issues you have covered – these can pick up extra marks if they are well used.
- Cover all topics in all the units you have studied when you are revising.
- If you make a point you must support it with either evidence or argument.
- In AE questions always refer back to the question to keep yourself relevant.

## A few do nots

- Do not answer all the questions in the exam booklets.
- Do not get confused between The Existence of God and Christianity: Belief and Science at Int 2.
- Do not miss out questions – always make an attempt.
- Do not write pages for questions worth only a few marks. A few lines are usually enough, although if your writing is the size of billboard writing, then a few pages might be required!
- In KU questions, be careful not to do analysis and evaluation. There is a high risk that you will not get any credit for it.
- In AE questions, try to avoid using KU-type information because you may not get marks for it if it is not relevant.
- In AE questions, do not write everything you know about a topic, unless it is a last resort.
- Do not panic. Take your time and do the questions you can do. Once you get started you often find that the flow of knowledge soon comes.

# IN CASE OF EMERGENCY

There are two emergencies that can happen in Higher and Int 2 RMPS: (a) you have no idea about how to answer a question (b) time is running out.

## What not to do

- Panic. Instead, leave a space, go on and do other questions that you can do.
- Leave. This is running away from the problem, once you leave the exam room it is all over for you.
- Miss a question out. If you write nothing you will get nothing. If you write something, then who knows what could happen?
- Phone a friend, go for 50/50 or ask the invigilators. There are rules against this somewhere.
- Stare. Do not sit and stare at the question, because that will only make you feel worse. You need to do something: either break the question down or move on to a new question or stick pins in the doll you have made of your RE teacher.
- Write a letter. Do not waste your time writing a wee letter to the marker explaining your predicament. Markers have hundreds of questions to mark and will not have the time to waste on your epistle.

## What to do

- Look back to see what topics you have already answered questions on. Whatever topic is missing, write anything about it that you know.

- If you do not understand a statement, try to write it down in your own words – do not just sit and stare at it. Do it word by word. Once you have done that, start writing your answer, but start by saying what you think the statement means. There's always the chance that your understanding of the statement is one way of looking at it.

- If you do not understand the meaning of words in a question, find a word or phrase in the question that you do understand and write about it. For example if 'human origins' is used, then just write all you know about Christian and evolutionary beliefs about human origins.

- If none of these works or applies, write anything about the topic – you never know, you might just get lucky.

## Out of time?

- Check that your desk is in the same time zone as the rest of the class or ask the invigilator if there is going to be any injury time.

- Write bullet points even for AE questions. They just have to be a brief summary of what you planned to write. Any writing that's in your exam book and not scored out by you will be marked and, if your information is correct, you will get some marks.

# AND FINALLY...

It is not often that you hear it from an adult, but you're going to hear it now, especially if an adult is reading this book to you as your bedtime story, which is highly likely. In this exam, you have permission to make a MESS of the AE questions. Here's how to do it:

> **M**ake a statement about the AE question or the quote that is used in it.
>
> **E**xplain what your statement means.
>
> **S**upport your statement with evidence.
>
> **S**upport your statement with arguments.

Remember this and you cannot go wrong. This idea is not mine. It was stolen from my colleague, Ms. C. Russell, who said I could use it if she got a "menshie" in the book.

# 3    Exemplar answers

## INTRODUCTION

This chapter looks at how to answer KU and AE questions. It would take a book on its own to give examples for every single topic that is covered in the exam so I have narrowed things down to the most popular options in each unit. Even if you do not study the topics in this chapter, you need to read the answers carefully and look at the comments on them because the techniques, features and comments can apply to every topic in the course.

We'll look at KU and AE answers from the following topics:

- Christianity: Belief and science
- Crime and punishment
- Gender issues
- Medical ethics
- War and peace
- World religions: Buddhism
- World religions: Christianity

# CHRISTIANITY: BELIEF AND SCIENCE

## Knowledge and Understanding sample answers
### Intermediate 2

> What do Christians mean by revelation?          **2 KU**
>
> (Int 2 Question (a) 2008)

### The Good

*Revelation is when people believe that something or someone comes to them with information from God. Sometimes people think that miracles are from God, such as the ones Jesus did during his life. He did the miracles to make a point about God's power.*

> Great start – you've told us what Christians mean by it.

> Now you've gone on to give an example of how revelation works. Very good technique.

This answer is good because it gets straight to the point with a clear definition and then goes on to give an example, which shows that the candidate knows exactly what Christians mean by revelation.

### The Bad

*Revelation is the Bible and other stuff God does.*

> You don't really know, do you? This is a guess but at least it's better than writing nothing at all. This might get a mark for stating that it is the Bible but it would only just scrape a mark.

Oh dear, oh dear, oh dear. Looks like this candidate has a very limited idea of what revelation means. One sentence written (and a short one at that), so there is no chance of this answer picking up more than one mark.

### The Ugly

*Christians mean that revelation is very important. It is a very important belief to Christians and they take it very seriously. Revelation is a belief Christians have and they agree that they should treat it with respect because of its importance.*

> Yes, it sure is.

> We know that, you've just told us – you're repeating yourself.

> You don't know what it is do you? You haven't actually said what it is at any point in your answer.

This is a terrible answer. It is what is technically known as 'drivel'. The candidate has not got a clue about revelation and so just rabbits on about its importance in the hope that the marker is in a generous mood. The answer says nothing and gets nothing. Beware: it is very easy to write an answer like this if you are struggling to remember something.

**Higher**

> What do Christians understand by revelation?   **4 KU**
>
> (Higher Question (a) 2009)

The Good

*There are two types of revelation. One type is general revelation and the other type is special revelation. Revelation means that God reveals something about himself that is hidden. God is so different from us that it is hard to work out that he is real just by looking at the world, so he reveals himself through general and special revelation. General revelation is sometimes called natural revelation. This is when we look at nature and work out it must have been designed and that God could be the designer. Special revelation is when God does something like tell people what to write in the Bible or come to earth, as Jesus, to show us what he is like and what he wants us to do.*

A mark here for telling us that there are two types. Good start.

A mark for the definition.

A good couple of sentences that would pick up more marks – you're on fire!

Now you're giving examples to give details of the facts you have stated – good technique.

And you've done the same with special revelation, except this time you have got all the information in one sentence – that's OK, you've said what it is and you then gone on to give an example of it.

A good answer that would get all four marks and more if that were possible. It could have been a little shorter but, nevertheless, it is what is being looked for. Try copying this answer out on a sheet of A4 paper to give you an idea of how long a four-mark KU answer needs to be.

The Bad

*Revelation is when God talks to human beings. One type of revelation is the Bible and all its stories and teachings. Another type of revelation is the universe because something had to put it here and it was God. People look at nature and see God in nature.*

> Not a good start – signs here that you do not know what you are talking about.

> OK, you seem to know that the Bible is a type of revelation, so you'd probably get a mark even though you did not say it was special revelation.

> You're talking around the idea of revelation rather than talking about it directly. There is enough here to suggest that you have a very basic idea of what natural revelation is.

A pretty sloppy answer isn't it? The candidate clearly has only a vague idea of what revelation is and gives what is really quite a poor answer. The most it would get is probably 2 marks.

The Ugly

*Revelation is a book in the Bible which God wrote. It is about how God will come and sort everyone out. There was a film made about it called the Exorcist and Damien had 666 on the back of his head, so revelation is when God comes to the world to judge everyone.*

> Oh no, what are you doing?

> Did you actually attend any RMPS classes?

> No it wasn't, it was *The Omen* – you can't even get the movie right!

This is the kind of answer that no RE teacher should ever be allowed to see since it would make him or her seriously doubt his or her ability to teach. The answer is totally irrelevant and completely misses the point. No marks here.

## Analysis and Evaluation sample answers

**Intermediate 2**

> 'The biblical account of creation should not be compared with scientific accounts of the beginning of the universe. Their purposes are quite different.' To what extent do you agree?    **8 AE**
>
> (Int 2 Question (b) 2003 – please note that the question was worth 10 marks in 2003, the maximum now is 8 marks)

The Good

I agree to a certain extent. The Bible is not a science book because there is no science in it. It would be wrong to compare it to science then because the two things are looking for different answers. The purpose of science is to tell us how the universe began not why. The Bible tells us why. The how and the why will give different answers. Their purposes are quite different. Another way their purposes are quite different is in the reasons the Bible writers wrote the Bible. They wrote it to tell us about God. Science people tell us about how things work. Some Christians do treat the Bible as a science book and say that it tells us how God made the world. I disagree with them because how can God make a universe in six days?

An excellent answer that would get something close to full marks. The first point is the best point because the candidate makes a point and then backs it up with reasons and examples. This shows the marker that you really understand the issue. Another good feature in this answer is that the candidate uses 'purposes are quite different' on two occasions. This helps to keep the answer focused and relevant.

Ah right, the warm-up that says nothing. Not a bad idea just to get you started to be honest. Won't get you marks but it may relax you.

A mark for this bit of analysis.

Even more information to back up your first point. You're up at four marks just now.

Well done, you made the statement in the previous sentence and now you are backing it up.

We know that – you've already told us.

Good point, very profound and another mark.

That's it! You've supported it with evidence. It's six!

Another good AE point, up at 5 marks. Now, let's back it up.

Another very good point that is worth a mark.

It's correct but you might not get the mark because of the repetition – a chance that you might though because you've used the same information to make a different point.

Oh bad luck, you ran out of steam. You've asked a rhetorical question, which, as a general rule, is a bad idea – it is you who has to answer questions, not the marker.

## The Bad

I agree that the Bible story of creation is a load of rubbish. Science gives facts about where the universe came from, but the Bible is just full of fairy stories about it. Science can prove that it is right, but religion can't. Science finds out how the universe was made and religion says why it is made. So I agree with the statement because the purposes are quite different, except that I think the purposes are very different and that they should not be compared because the Bible is not a science book.

> Ouch! Bad start. This is not what the statement is about and it is rarely a good sign when candidates write words like 'load of rubbish' – it puts markers on a 'rant alert'.

> Badly put but it might get a mark because it is saying that the Bible cannot be trusted.

> Back on topic again. A mark here for the point made.

> A bold statement but it is off topic.

> Finally, a reference to the statement and a mark for the final point.

This answer would be lucky to get much more than 3 out of 8. It is rant. In an examination room there is an angry teenage atheist writing this answer – you can almost hear the pen scraping the top of the desk. Try to avoid rants if you can. They are usually very one-sided and do not answer the question. This candidate hits the target from time to time but, from reading this answer, you know that this person has not taken the time to sit back and think about the two or three points they were going to make.

## The Ugly

Why do people always have a go at religion? I am a Christian and I get fed up with people slagging off the Bible. It is up to me what I believe and, if we believe that the Bible is right, then, that is up to us. Science gets things wrong as well. The Bible tells us that God made a good universe, but science only tells us how it works. So, I think the purpose of science and religion is different and that they should leave each other alone.

> Oh! Look! A mark!

> Eh? What are you on about? Totally irrelevant answer.

This is a nightmare of an answer. The candidate does not seem to know what the statement is about and by sheer chance manages to scrape a mark.

There are lots of things wrong with the answer. It does not answer the question. It contains a personal plea on behalf of the whole of Christianity to lay off it. The one reference to the statement shows that the candidate does not really get it.

**Higher**

> 'Evolutionary theory has removed the need for a designer of the universe.' How successfully do Christians respond to this challenge? **10 AE**
>
> (Higher Question (h) 2008 – was worth 4 KU and 6 AE but we'll just say it is worth 10 AE to show you how to write a full AE answer)

The Good

This is a controversial statement. Christians have been quite successful in responding to it. There are three main groups of Christians and their responses to this challenge are different. The first thing I need to explain is what the challenge is. This statement is saying that the universe is all down to a mix of luck and natural laws. This means that the universe does not have a purpose. The literalist group of Christians see this as a challenge to their beliefs because they believe that God did design the universe and that he designed it in the way the Bible describes. Their response to the challenge is to say that evolution did not happen. This is a weak response because the evidence for evolution is so great that there is a good chance that it is a fact. It could be a strong response because you could argue that evolution is not a scientific fact yet – it is still a theory.

The warm-up.

Well done, showing you know that there is more than one Christian view.

Excellent tactic.

Two good sentences: you explain the statement and, then, you go on to explain the problem. At least a mark in here.

Excellent section. You've stated their view, then explained the problem, given their response and, then, said whether the response was strong or weak. At least three marks in this bit.

The second group of Christians are Intelligent Design Christians. Their scientists at the

Discovery Institute say that evolution is natural but that God fine-tuned it to produce life like ours. They say that something as complex as the universe could not be the result of pure chance. This is a successful response because it uses scientific discoveries and does not make itself look stupid by saying that all evolution is wrong. It could be a weak response because it is trying to mix science and religion and use the God of the Gaps to explain things science cannot explain.

> Reference to an organisation – should pick up a mark or two if it is well used.

> Same as above – see the way you have kept the same structure for tackling the second Christian view – that's the way to do it. At least three marks in this too.

The third group of Christians are the liberal Christians. They would say that the universe needs a Designer and that evolution is God's way of designing. Alistair McGrath and other leading Christians argue that evolution actually gives more evidence for a Designer. Their response is successful because, just like the middle group, they take science on board and change their view of God to keep in line with science. Some people say that, because of this, their response to the challenge is weak because they have to keep changing their view of God.

> Another source – could be worth something if it is well used.

> Same formula, same result, at least three marks.

So, overall, the three Christian groups have different views and I think the last group is the most successful.

> Conclusion was not so good but you have been drawing conclusions throughout.

This is how you answer AE questions. This is a really disciplined approach because the candidate has got a simple formula for the structure: **explain the statement – explain the issue then state a position – explain the position – strengths – weaknesses – conclusion.** That has been done three times and the marks have been steadily built up. It's almost as if the candidate wrote three mini-essays. By breaking the question down like this, rather than doing it in one big mouthful, the whole thing has become more manageable.

## The Bad

Christians are not successful in answering this challenge. They think that God designed the universe and that he made it like it says in the Bible. This is a bad idea because why does God allow people to suffer in evolution? Christians do not accept that some things might not need to be designed. It could be that we just like to think the universe is designed to make us feel a bit better rather than it all being luck. If Christians said that evolution was used by God to make the universe then, maybe, people would listen to them more and they could respond successfully to the challenge. Some Christians do believe in evolution and say that the Bible is just a myth. This is a successful response because it shows that some Christians will listen to what science says and this will make them more modern and acceptable.

> Bad sign – you are generalising; there is more than one Christian view and you should show that you know that whenever you get the chance.

> A mark here because this is the view of at least some Christians.

> There's maybe a mark in these two sentences but the problem is that you have not referred to the statement early enough in your answer and you have left yourself open to straying off the point.

> Where on earth are you going with this point? Look at the statement in the question!

> Good, there's the making of a point in here. Now you need to build upon it – but the next sentence shows that you have not.

> Maybe a mark in the last two sentences because you show that some Christians do disagree with a biblical view of creation and that has some implications for there being a designer.

This answer would probably get around 4 out of 10. The first thing to notice is that there is a generalisation and this is often a sign that the candidate does not have a full grasp of what Christianity is about. The second thing is that there is no structure. It is difficult to follow the candidate's line of thought. The candidate does make a couple of good points but, because there is no structure, these points are wasted. If they were developed even a little then this answer could have scored a couple of marks more.

## The Ugly

I think that evolution proves that there is no designer. Evolution shows that things can change in small ways over time and that they only appear to be designed when they are not. There is no proof that there is a god or

> Don't care what you think – you were asked a different kind of question altogether.

> No proof? Where have you been all year? There are proofs, it's just that you do not accept them.

> A charitable mark for this maybe, just so you don't get a big fat zero.

a designer and evolution shows this is true. Richard Dawkins says 'Truth is scientific truth' and Albert Einstein said 'Religion without science is lame and science without religion is blind.' This shows that there is no Designer because there is no proof.

> Great stuff – quotes. Not so great – you've just stuck them in to use up space. They both mean nothing.

This is dire. It is unlikely that the candidate would score any marks for this. Possibly in the second sentence the candidate would stumble upon a mark. The candidate has also given a personal view – the questions ask for a personal view of how successful Christians have been in responding to the challenge, not your own view of the challenge. So many candidates have done this over the years. The candidate says there is 'no proof' of God's existence. Try to avoid writing that. It is wrong: there is proof of the existence of God, which some people accept and some people do not accept. If there were 'no proof', then we could not even have the debate. In any case, using phrases like 'no proof' makes the answer sound like a bit of a rant.

# CRIME AND PUNISHMENT

## Knowledge and Understanding sample answers
### Intermediate 2

> What is meant by a deterrent?
>
> **2 KU**
> (Int 2 Question (a) 2009)

### The Good

A deterrent is a purpose of punishment. This is when a punishment is given to put people off doing crimes. It is like setting an example. Putting people in prison for life for doing a murder is meant to put off other people from

> Well done, you have said what it is.

> Now you have explained it a bit, so that could also be worth a mark.

murdering because they will think that they would not want to go to jail for life

> And now you have gone on and given an example. This is always a good way to 'pad out' your answers.

Good answer because for everything that is named there is a description.

## The Bad

Deterrent = stopping others from doing crimes.

> Too vague!

This may or may not get a mark because it is so vague – the description could apply to any of the purposes of punishment.

## The Ugly

A deterrent is somebody who is a teenager and does crimes.

> No, that is a **delinquent**, which is something you might become if you do not understand what a deterrent is.

This is just wrong.

## Higher

> Describe two sentences that might be given to criminals in UK courts. **4 KU**
>
> (Higher Question 2 (a) SQP)

## The Good

Fines: a fine is when the court decides that a crime is not serious enough for the person to go to jail. The criminal has to pay money to the court for the crime they have committed. Fines can be anything from a few pounds to thousands of pounds.

> Not 100% accurate, but accurate enough to get you something – sometimes it is not appropriate to send a person to jail.

> Simple but effective description of what happens.

> And the little bit of extra detail does not do any harm.

Jail: people in the UK can be jailed for more serious crimes. This means that they are kept in prison and are not allowed to be free until they have earned their freedom or served their sentence.

> Good start because you are making it clear it is for more serious crimes.

> Fair enough – yes it is pretty basic but questions like this are designed to relax you.

The style isn't brilliant, but the answer scores marks. Each sentence gets a couple of lines of explanation and that makes sure of the marks.

### The Bad

You can get community service which is a waste of time because you do not have to go and it is difficult to chase you up if you don't go. You can also go to jail where you are kept in a cell until you have done all of your time.

> You name the punishment and then you give an opinion of it. No thanks for your opinion: you were not asked for it – we wanted a description.

> The jail description would get something – a rather naff answer.

Sounds like this candidate is speaking from personal experience! Main problem, here, is that the candidate gives opinions and that is not what was asked for. Descriptions only for this kind of question.

### The Ugly

You can be executed by the prison which is when you are killed. You can also be put on probation.

> Oh really? In the UK? Er, no!

> This is correct but you have just named it – you need to describe what it involves.

The first point is wrong and the second point simply names and gives no details. No marks.

## Analysis and Evaluation sample answers

### Intermediate 2

Explain the advantages and disadvantages of making sure the punishment fits the crime.    **8 AE**

(Int 2 Question (g) 2010)

### The Good

There are many advantages of making sure the punishment fits the crime. The first advantage

> Excellent, using a phrase from the question right away. Good idea, helps keep you on track.

> Good – you are numbering your advantages and that gives your answer shape and direction.

is that people might feel protected because the criminal has been put away. He could have attacked someone, so it is only right that he should lose his freedom in case he attacks another person. Another advantage is that, if a criminal murders someone in the USA, he can get executed. This is an advantage because the killer will never kill again and people will feel that it is like an eye for an eye so that his punishment fits the crime.

Good point.

And you follow up with an example, excellent!

Not sure where this is going.

Ah right, well done, I see where you are going.

And you go on and describe the effect of it – good.

Some people do not agree with this view. A disadvantage could be that, if we do to the criminal what he has done to another person, we are just as bad as the criminal. Another disadvantage is that innocent people could suffer. Like when a man kills someone and he is executed to make it a life for a life, but did not actually commit the crime, then, making the punishment fit the crime has a bad result.

Good intro to the opposite side. Always a good idea to keep a balance because you can usually say more.

Good point, shame that you did not give an example.

Interesting.

Good point and example.

I think you have to be careful when you say this because it has advantages and disadvantages.

Aye, well, getting tired aren't we? This says nothing.

**This is a very good answer. It is not especially long but it is direct and straight to the point. Examples to highlight the points are given throughout. That is what the SQA is looking for.**

## The Bad

The punishment should fit the crime because that is justice. If you do something wrong to someone, then you should get the same thing done to you, but that might be bad because somebody has to do the wrong thing back to you and they might become a criminal too. One reason for doing this is it makes people feel better or protected and that is why the

Interesting.

After sixteen readings, I get the point and it is not a bad one.

OK fair point.

punishment should fit the crime. A disadvantage
is sometimes the punishment does not work,
it is the wrong kind of punishment and the
criminal does not improve because of it.

> Yes, this is OK – I get the drift – retribution might not help the criminal's situation, fair point. Would have helped if you referred back to the question.

This answer talks around the issue rather than talk about it. A couple of good points are made but the candidate never gets to the stage where you feel that he or she is on top of the issue. Main problem here is that the candidate seems to have lost the thread of the question.

## The Ugly

The punishment should always fit the crime
because that is what the court is for. It
decides that the punishment fits the crime and
nobody else. When the punishment does not fit

> Eh?

> Eh?

the crime, there are many disadvantages and
advantages like it is not nice to get revenge
on people and that is bad for the world. The
punishment should not fit the crime because
we are not like we used to be and execute for
no reason because we try to help criminals
now.

> OK, you might get something here for this point but you are waffling.

> You might get something here too but this really is pretty weak showing that you have not really got a clue about what you are talking about.

It's an Int 2 answer, Jim, but not as we know it. A lot of waffle, which markers can see straight through. This candidate has loads of words that are right, but little in the way of clear and argued points.

### Higher

'All methods of execution are immoral.'  **8 AE**

How might a non religious person respond to this view?

(Higher Question (c) 2007)

## The Good

The statement means that, it does not matter what kind of execution is carried out, it is still wrong. A lot depends on what you believe about the death penalty. If you believe that the death penalty is wrong, then it does not matter what method is chosen. It is wrong. As one opponent in Texas put it, 'This is premeditated, carefully thought out ceremonial killing.' This statement suggests that it is wrong because it is planned and because there is the ceremony of the trial, the appeals and the build up to the execution itself.

*Good start, showing that you know what the statement means.*

*No problem with this, good point.*

There are different opinions about the death penalty being moral. In the US some campaigners argue that the death penalty is a cruel and unusual punishment. If it is cruel and unusual, then you could say that it is immoral. The problem is that what I might say is cruel and unusual another person might say is ok. Executions could also be immoral because, it does not matter what method is used, a human is taking the life of another human and that is wrong. How can killing a killer for killing be moral? There are examples from every type of execution of it going wrong and the person suffering. There are more examples of innocent people being executed and if that is not immoral then what is? Whatever method of execution is used the criminal has to wait for a long time for his death to come. That means he is being deliberately made to suffer or fight for his life – that is cruel and since it does not happen to a lot of people it is also unusual. So that makes the method of execution immoral.

*Good use of quote and it has also been explained to show how it connects with the question.*

*Good point and very useful to refer to a situation in real life.*

*Clocking up these marks now!*

*Good question but you did not take it anywhere. Try to avoid rhetorical questions.*

*Know what you're trying to say but it doesn't really come off does it?*

*OK, you had to work it a wee bit here and then twist it round to fit the question but you did it well.*

On the other hand some non religious people think execution is a good idea and that lethal injection is the moral way to do it. Most states in the US use lethal injection because it does not cause the prisoner any pain. This is a moral method because it is humane. The prisoner is just put to sleep. It might not be nice to put someone to sleep, but it does not make it an immoral method. Some people might even argue that not to make the criminal suffer is immoral. The criminal caused suffering, so, to be morally fair, you have to make sure that he suffers as much as the victim. You could say that certain methods of execution are immoral because they involve making the prisoner deliberately suffer and that to make people suffer is immoral because we should be trying to protect each other from unnecessary suffering.

> Well done, keeping on track by mentioning phrase from the question. This whole bit would get a mark or so.

> Good point and it might get something; it would definitely have got something if you had gone on and explained it a bit.

> Unusual angle to take but perfectly relevant.

> Good point too but why did you stop there? You could have rounded the whole thing off nicely with a final conclusion.

**Wow! This covers the key issues and the candidate knows exactly what she wants to say. Every point is supported with evidence and the candidate has shown a terrific awareness of both sides of the argument. At 450 words long, it is about the right length for a 10 mark answer.**

## The Bad

The death penalty is wrong because you could end up executing an innocent person. You could get the wrong person and put them through all that suffering for something they did not do, that is why the death penalty is wrong. Deathpenaltyinfo.org says that executions are wrong because the different methods can go wrong and can make the criminal suffer more pain than they were meant to. Some people,

> This is not what the question was about. Read it again! You are off track!

> Hello-oh! You're still off track. Go back and read the question before it is too late.

> Phew! Getting back on track and with a source as well. Good stuff.

who agree with the death penalty, might feel that lethal injection is the only right way to treat a criminal because it is humane and involves no pain, whereas other methods of execution can involve a huge amount of pain for the criminal.

> Well on track now and possibly a couple of marks here for you.

People, who are against the death penalty, would say that all methods of execution are immoral because to take a person's life for any reason is immoral. Just because a person has murdered someone doesn't mean that we, then, have the right to kill him. If we do not have the right to kill, then no method of execution can be moral.

> Taking the opposite view ... good tactic. Another mark here.

> Another mark for this point too. This is borderline overall and you made it borderline because you started off by not answering the question. Once you have written your first point for any question, look back at the question, read what you have written and make sure it is relevant.

**Good to see an attempt to use sources – that can always pick up marks. Several good points made but the problem is that they have not been supported with evidence or argument. It's a mistake to leave statements unsupported.**

The Ugly

If you take a life you should lose your life. I think the execution is right because why should a person live when they have killed someone else? They have taken someone's life, so they have given up the right to have their own life. I think that if people were executed for crimes apart from murder that would be wrong. People like drug addicts need to be helped and not executed. Crimes like robbery should mean that people get put in jail. Life imprisonment can work, but only as long as it means life. I think that the death penalty is less cruel than life imprisonment because imagine being in prison for your whole life and never having the chance to get out again. So yes, I think that non religious people would think that methods of execution are immoral.

> Wrong approach! Read the question!

> Maybe a wee smidgen of a mark here but you're still off track.

> What are you on about? You have not mentioned the question once. You're going on about other punishments. This is about the **death penalty** – it is not a chance for you to have a rant.

> Woop! At last, a mention of the question but dear oh dear oh dear it's almost impossible to see how what you wrote before had anything to do with the question. Marks thrown away here.

31

This is a rant. It is a personal rant against the justice system in the UK. Problem is, the answer is off the topic as a result. Avoid ranting at all costs.

# GENDER ISSUES

## Knowledge and Understanding sample answers
**Intermediate 2**

> Describe **two** historic roles of men in the family.      **4 KU**
>
> (Int 2 Question (b) SQP)

### The Good

*One historic role is that the man goes out to work. He is the breadwinner which means that his role is to provide for his family. Another historic role is that the man is the head of the home. This means that men were the decision makers in the home about things like schooling, money and discipline of the children.*

> Good explanation

> A repeat performance – this is how KU should be done.

**Good answer because for everything that is named there is a description.**

### The Bad

*The man is in charge at home and it is his job to go out and earn money for the family. This has changed and it is much more equal now because many women go out to work.*

> Fair enough – gets a mark.

> Might struggle to get something here because what is being described is not necessarily historic. Careless.

**Might get a couple of marks but probably no more because the second point is not historic.**

The Ugly

Men do real work and women only do housework, that is a historic role.

Aye, well ... must have been off school that day.

> Under no circumstances repeat this in public! It is both wrong and inaccurate.

## Higher

Describe **two** gender issues affecting the UK today.  **4 KU**

(Higher Question (c) 2009)

The Good

One gender issue is that of equality. There are several issues under this heading. Equality can be about equal pay, which is getting the same pay for the same work—which is the law, but which is not the practice. Also under this heading is equal opportunities in relation to promotion and the existence of the glass ceiling which prevents women from making their way up the promotion ladder. The second issue is to do with the way the media portrays men and women. There is stereotyping and in particular the use of the female body to promote products which is considered to be a form of exploitation.

**Not full marks but enough to get a decent mark. Second issue is weaker than the first.**

> You've named it, now explain it.

> Good point.

> Another one. Good work.

> Useful idea to help you keep count.

> Probably only one mark in here because you have not given an explanation of more than one thing.

The Bad

Two issues are stereotyping and equal pay. Stereotyping is when men and women are portrayed in certain roles, e.g. the woman is the sexy one or housewife and the man is the protector and breadwinner.

> Good start. A mark for explaining stereotyping and a mark for the example.

Where's the equal pay information? You blew it –
this could have got four marks.

## The Ugly

Stereotyping is a terrible thing. Men and
women should not be stereotyped because it is
not truly how they are. Some people stereotype
people by the race they are in, like Scotsmen
wearing tartan and eating porridge all the
time.

> Nope, me neither, no idea what this has to do with the question.

Oh dear, oh dear, oh dear ... this is a rant!

# Analysis and Evaluation sample answers

## Intermediate 2

> Explain the advantages **and** disadvantages of encouraging
> gender rights.          **8 AE**
>
> (Int 2 Question (g) 2010)

## The Good

There are many advantages of encouraging
gender rights. The first advantage is that
people might feel that they are being treated
equally. Women will feel valued because they
are being seen as the same as men at work and
at home. Another advantage is that women
could feel that they can have ambitions and
that the glass ceiling is not going to prevent
their path to promotion. This is an advantage
because there are many talented women who
have missed out on promotion because of
their sex. Gender equality in this means that
employers have a better chance of employing
the best PERSON for the job rather than the
best MAN for the job.

> Good – you are numbering your advantages and that gives your answer shape and direction.

> First rate; makes points and supports them. At least four marks in here.

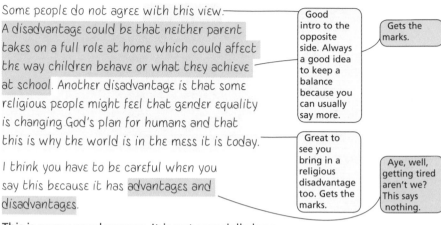

Some people do not agree with this view. A disadvantage could be that neither parent takes on a full role at home which could affect the way children behave or what they achieve at school. Another disadvantage is that some religious people might feel that gender equality is changing God's plan for humans and that this is why the world is in the mess it is today.

I think you have to be careful when you say this because it has advantages and disadvantages.

> Good intro to the opposite side. Always a good idea to keep a balance because you can usually say more.

> Gets the marks.

> Great to see you bring in a religious disadvantage too. Gets the marks.

> Aye, well, getting tired aren't we? This says nothing.

This is a very good answer. It is not especially long but it is direct and straight to the point. Examples to highlight the points are given throughout. That is what the SQA is looking for.

## The Bad

Gender equality has advantages. Everyone should be treated equally, whether male or female, because this means that everyone is able to use the talents they have. A disadvantage is that society might suffer because the mother is not at home to look after the children and this could cause problems at school.

> Excellent, gets the marks.

> Contentions, but the argument has been made.

Too short. Gets half marks but you are not going to get 8 marks for writing about five lines.

## The Ugly

I disagree with the question. There are no disadvantages in gender equality. Everything is a plus like equal chances to get jobs and not being stereotyped in the media. Girls will not be pressured to look like supermodels. They wear their plunging necklines and short skirts

> Uh-oh. Rant alert!

> You're not asked to do this. Do what the question tells you.

and men just see them as sex objects but that is wrong because there is more to women than that.

**Do what the question tells you, not what you want it to tell you!**

> You might get a couple of marks from a kind-hearted marker here but you just haven't tackled the question.

### Higher

> Explain **two** religious concerns about current gender issues in the UK.                                                    **6 AE**
>
> (Higher Question (e) 2010)

### The Good

A lot depends on whether or not you have a traditional view of women. Some religious people who have a traditional view of women will be concerned because they believe that we are upsetting the role that God had planned. This could apply to some Christian groups – the Amish for example have this view and give women a very traditional role and they actually live separately from the rest of society to make sure that the traditions are kept on. It might also be applied to some Muslim countries too where women have limited rights. In some Muslim communities in the UK women have a subordinate role and it can also be seen in some Jewish communities too where young women might feel pressured to move away from their traditional roles.

More progressive religious people will be very concerned about the porn industry. For them women are treated like sex objects and sex is treated like a game rather than a gift from

> Excellent point that would get a mark.

> Good example, a shame they are not in the UK – no marks.

> Couple of marks in here but could do with better examples.

> Traditional religious people will be too, but the point is worth a mark.

> Couple of marks in here too. Good recovery after a ropey start.

God. The porn industry devalues women and men and reduces them simply to physical beings rather than gifts from God.

This answer stumbles across 5 out of 6 marks by accident. Take care to write about the UK and not other countries – you will not get marks for that kind of mistake.

## The Bad

Religions have many concerns about gender issues in the UK. They hate the way sex is used in the media and see it as a major problem because it treats men and women as sex objects and it also reinforces stereotypes. They are also concerned because God made everyone equal, but; even although there is a law in the UK to stop unequal treatment, it still goes on and this is a major concern because God's creations are not being treated fairly.

> Good point – gets a mark but to get a second mark it needs to expand on the second point in the sentence.

> Couple of marks in here because you have explained the issue with two examples.

First point not so good, second point is good – you needed to do that both times.

## The Ugly

Religions should not be concerned about gender issues because it is none of their business. They created the problem and so they should just keep their noses out of it and not cause any more trouble because we are sick of them. Religions cause nothing but harm, including wars and terrorism, and they should just stick to believing in God (even although there isn't one) and let ordinary people deal with moral problems.

> Ah, got out of the wrong side of the bed this morning.

This is a rant. It is a personal rant at religion and anything else that happens to get in the way.

# MEDICAL ETHICS

## Knowledge and Understanding sample answers

**Intermediate 2**

> Describe **two** circumstances in which euthanasia might be requested.
>
>            **4 KU**
>
> (Int 2 Question (b) SQP)

### The Good

Euthanasia might be requested if a patient is terminally ill and they feel that the pain has got to a stage where they can take no more and decide to ask the doctor to give them medication which will kill them. Another time could be when someone is in a car crash and is badly injured. The doctors, after talking to the family, might agree that the best thing to do is to give the patient drugs to take away any pain, but which also kill the patient.

> Good point – gets a couple of marks

> Good point again.

**Good answer because for everything that is named there is a description.**

### The Bad

I would want euthanasia if I could not take the pain any more. Euthanasia can be voluntary, non voluntary, active and passive and you can have different combinations of these. People, who have strokes, can sometimes be given non voluntary euthanasia because of their poor prognosis. People, who have massive heart attacks, could get the same if their chances are poor. It is illegal in the UK, but legal in Holland.

> It's a circumstance but at Int 2 more is required.

> Not circumstances!

> At last, a mark!

> Another example and another mark.

> Irrelevant.

**An easy question and a very messy answer. All over the place isn't it?**

The Ugly

*Euthanasia is against the law so it can never ever be requested.*

> It can be. It's just that it can't be given.

**This is dire.**

## Higher

> Describe **two** uses of embryos.                    **4 KU**
>
> (Higher Question (c) 2010)

The Good

*Embryo use all stems from IVF so one use of embryos is that of IVF. Out of IVF come more uses. The most obvious one is to allow people to have children through IVF treatment. This process can be used for a variety of reasons including assisting couples who have difficulty conceiving or selecting embryos without particular defects. Another use of embryos is research. Through IVF, embryos are created and can have research done on them by scientists for up to fifteen days after which they should be destroyed.*

> Yip, worth a mark.

> Named and described – gets a couple of marks.

> Same again.

**Clear and to the point.**

The Bad

*Embryos can be used for research. This is where scientists can carry out experiments to help understand reproduction or genetic diseases. They have to destroy them after a couple of weeks.*

> Named and described – good.

**Half marks for this – there's more than just this.**

The Ugly

*Research*

*Saviour siblings*

> Is that it? No marks for listing.

**Three words for four marks? Dream on.**

# Analysis and Evaluation sample answers

## Intermediate 2

> 'It is acceptable to legalise euthanasia because it ends human life.'
>
> How far might religious people agree with this statement?
> Give reasons for your answer.       **8 AE**
>
> (Int 2 Question (f) 2008))

## The Good

Most religious leaders will come out against this statement so they would disagree with it. The reasons they are against legalising euthanasia is because God gives life and only God can take it away. It is not up to the state to decide who lives and who dies, this is a decision that only God can make. Another reason they would be unhappy about it is that it makes it legal to kill another person. They would say that euthanasia is killing, nothing else, just killing and in the Bible it says in the Ten Commandments that we should not kill. Another reason is that the law gets us on a slippery slope. If we take away the right of people not to be killed then what next? Do we euthanise people because they are no longer useful and not just because they are in pain? This leads to devaluing human life. Just because we are suffering, we should not think that the suffering is worthless nor should we think that our life is worthless. All of these things have value according to religious people.

*[Margin notes:]*
- OK. Now tell us!
- Well done, at least a couple of marks here.
- And again!
- Hat trick of great ideas.
- Full house, great ideas.

**Perfect!**

## The Bad

*Christians would be against this statement although personally some Christians might be in favour of it. Legalising euthanasia is just like legalising killing, which the Bible says is wrong. Jesus suffered on the cross and did not complain so we should be prepared to suffer and not complain about it as well. The slippery slope argument is also against legalising euthanasia.*

> Well said – marks for this.

> Might get something but there is a need to explain it a bit more.

> Aye, so it is but you need to tell us why.

This answer talks around the issue rather than talks about it. A couple of good points are made, but the candidate never gets to the stage where you feel that he or she is on top of the issue.

## The Ugly

*I disagree with the question. There should be a law allowing euthanasia. Margo MacDonald MSP is right – we should not be forced to live a life that we do not want to live. Religious people would be unhappy about this statement because they say that God chooses when we live and die not us. Well, I don't think so actually – it is our life and we live it as we want and anyway we don't even know that there is a God anyway.*

> Fair enough, gets something.

> What are you on about? It's about euthanasia, not existence of God!

Pretty poor – there's really only one point made, this rest is just pure havering.

## Higher

> Explain **two** drawbacks of IVF.            **8 AE**
> (Higher Question 2 (b) SQP)

## The Good

The first drawback of IVF is related to the embryo itself. The status of the embryo is unclear. Some people see the embryo as a person, some a non-person and some a potential person. If you see the embryo as a person, then it is clear that you are working with a human being—which is the view of Pope John Paul II, which has later been endorsed by the present pope. If the embryo is a non-person, then there is not really an issue because you are not dealing with a human being and, if it is a potential person, very clear rules about what you can and cannot do are required so that the rights of the potential person are not infringed.

> First key point.

> Well explained – a mark so far

> Mark for the example.

> Mark for the example.

> Mark for the example.

A second drawback relates to what can be done with the embryo. There are drawbacks of allowing scientists to do what they like because that could lead to the creation of monsters. There could be drawbacks related to creating saviour siblings which could be seen as exploiting an innocent person or allowing people to create designer babies rather than taking their chances.

> Setting up the second key point.

> Overstated but we get the idea – gets a mark.

> Point well made.

**Bit short on the second point but enough to get 6 or 7 out of 8. A very good answer.**

## The Bad

One drawback of IVF is that it is only successful one in three times which is why the NHS gives couples only three goes to have a baby. Another drawback is designer babies because people should not be allowed to choose what baby they have because this makes the baby a product and not a human being. The bad side is that IVF might be killing a person.

> 1 mark for this.

> Fair point but needs more explaining – maybe a mark.

> Good point, worth a mark.

Why did this candidate not write more? This could have been a really good answer if they wrote more. Eight marks available – going to get that for three lines? No!

The Ugly

IVF has good points and bad points. Good points are that it lets childless couples have babies and let's face it everyone has the right to have a baby if they want to have one. Another good point is that saviour siblings can be made like in My Sister's Keeper.

> Gets a mark for explaining the point.

> Doesn't get any marks – no explanation. But it is a good movie!

Sloppy answer – looks like this person was in a rush to leave the exam room.

# WAR AND PEACE

## Knowledge and Understanding sample answer
**Intermediate 2**

> Explain **two** arguments in favour of possessing WMDs. **4 KU**
> (Int 2 Question (b) 2008)

The Good

WMDs are weapons of mass destruction and they include chemical, biological and nuclear weapons. There are many arguments in favour of possessing such weapons. The two main arguments are deterrence and self defence.

> Well done, well organised answer.

1. By possessing these weapons, countries are showing that they are prepared to use them in retaliation for any attack made on them by other countries. The UK's possession of nuclear weapons, for example, puts off other countries from firing theirs at us because

> Gets a mark.

> Great stuff – 2 marks for this paragraph.

we could simply fire back with the same kind of weapons.

2. By having WMDs the government is fulfilling its duty to protect its citizens. If we did not have WMDs, then that could leave us open to attacks. For example, if Kuwait had nuclear weapons when Saddam Hussein attacked, we could ask the question, would he have attacked; by having WMDs the state could have protected its people. As it turned out, they could not because they didn't have much to defend themselves with.

> Gets a mark.

> Great use of examples.

An answer to die for. Magic.

## The Bad

Deterrence – having WMDs put other people off using them. A drawback of this is the cost of buying and maintaining the weapons.

> Probably a couple of marks here. One for saying what it is and one for explaining it.

Protection – they protect people

> Hmmm, at best a mark. Should have been done like the first point.

No excuse for this kind of answer. The first part is fine but the second part is really too brief. It needs a bit more to get full marks.

## The Ugly

WMDs are immoral, so there are no arguments in favour of having them. I mean how can anyone argue in favour of nuclear bombs when they cause 500 mph winds, firestorms, fall out, cancer and death? They are disgusting and I think nobody should have them.

> Question is looking for facts not opinions.

This is a rant. Even if you disagree with possessing WMDs, there are some people who might prefer to have them, and you need to write down what their arguments are.

**Higher**

> In what ways do United Nations (UN) conventions promote peace?
>
> **6 KU**
>
> (Higher Question (d) 2009)

## The Good

There are many UN conventions that deal with war and promote peace. Behind all of the conventions is the idea that war should always be a last resort. The UN enforces its conventions to try to get the opposing nations together to find ways of avoiding conflict through diplomacy so the conventions promote diplomacy as the way to solve problems, not attack. The Geneva Conventions contain UN approaches to war and these are not designed to prevent war, but when it happens to protect people as best they can.

> A point here because that is the aim of many of the conventions.

> Good explanation of the point, which is worth another mark.

> Not obviously relevant but in protecting people there is a suggestion of promoting peace. Possible mark here.

They promote peace because they offer alternatives to war through things like trade sanctions which are designed to force warring countries to the negotiating table to resolve the problem. It also enforces international laws on war which, again, can make countries think twice before they go to war because if they are found to have broken the law, then they risk being brought to justice for crimes against humanity.

> Good point and good to see an example.

> Again there are marks in here, probably a couple because you have expanded on the point.

It is a good but not a brilliant answer to what is a tough area in the course.

> Got the wrong end of the stick here. A convention can be an agreement as well as a large gathering of people. In this case it is an agreement.

## The Bad

UN Conventions meet whenever there is the threat of war. They make people look for other

> Back on track here – this is right.

ways to solve problems rather than just going to war. The Security Council meets and tries to force the enemies to talk to each other and find a peaceful way out of the situation. The Geneva conventions also help promote peace because they have rules about how to fight the war and because the rules have to be obeyed think it is not worth the hassle of going to war.

> Fair point and worth a mark.

This candidate looks as they know a reasonable amount but they haven't done that in the answer. What a pity!

### The Ugly

UN Conventions prevent wars all the time by making people follow them. There are Geneva conventions, which try to limit war, and the Security Council, who meet to try and stop wars from happening and get enemies talking instead which promotes peace.

> Not sure that this is entirely true.

> OK, this would get a mark.

Very sketchy stuff. If the candidate had tried to write a bit more information on the facts rather than simply state them this could have got more.

## Analysis and Evaluation sample answers

**Intermediate 2**

> 'A pacifist response is the best response to war.'
> Do you agree? Give reasons for your answer    **6 AE**
>
> (Int 2 Question (d) SQP)

### The Good

I agree and disagree with the statement. It is the best response to war because it means that people will not go around killing other people.

> A fine tactic – gives you more to say rather than just stating one side of the argument.

> Point is well made here, definitely two marks.

You cannot have a war if nobody turns up, and if everybody was a pacifist, then that is what would happen. That is not what happens but, as long as we have people who are pacifists, it is a good response because it makes people think about whether wars and killing are right.

I disagree with the statement because no pacifist has ever won a war and that could have meant people like Hitler, Pol Pot and Hussein continuing to kill their own people. Individuals like these men do not bother about pacifists, they are only interested in keeping in power and not worried about morality.

> Well done. You state your point and then you explain it. 2 marks.

A lot depends on the situation. Pacifism might be a good idea if the war is being fought far away, but if you are fighting for your own freedom then pacifism is a position that is not going to win a lot of supporters because people will naturally want to protect themselves. So, I think my view is mixed. Pacifism is both a good and bad response to war.

> And more of the same – brilliant!

This is a very good answer. It is not especially long but it is direct and straight to the point. Examples to highlight the points are given throughout. That is what the SQA is looking for.

The Bad

Pacifism is the coward's way out. It is not the best response to war. I mean what happens if your country is invaded. Do you sit back and say, 'Oh hello, welcome to my country, do come in and have a wee cup of tea and a Tunnock's Caramel Log?' I don't think anyone should be doing that. You have to fight for your freedom.

> Certainly worth a mark, maybe two.

World War II was not won by pacifism – it was won by fighting to defend our freedom and to win back the freedom of others. Simply saying to Hitler that we would rather he didn't invade Poland and bomb London and can we talk about it was not going to save anyone.

> Good example and a very good point. Worth two marks.

A borderline answer. It might get 4 out of 6 at a push. The first point could have been made a bit better.

### The Ugly

Wars are wrong and pacifism is the only response there should be. I would never kill anyone and I don't think I should be forced to. I even felt bad when I had to flush Glennie the goldfish down the pan at home so no I would not fight and that is why pacifism is the best response to war. Any other response is just making matters worse.

> Nah, this is going nowhere. You are too busy mourning the demise of Glennie – just a hint of taking the rip out of the exam – does not do you any favours. Nul points.

Shocker! This person is in the exam for a carry on. Avoid doing this kind of thing. N.B.: no animals were harmed in the writing of this answer.

### Higher

> Explain **two** drawbacks of going to war.     8 AE
>
> (Higher Question 2 (b) SQP)

### The Good

One drawback of going to war is that it is going to cost money and it is going to cost lives. Cost is a huge problem in the middle of a recession and cutbacks. The money for war has to come from somewhere and if it comes from somewhere then other things have to suffer. Human lives are lost in war. That is

> Excellent point. A mark for stating the point and a mark for its expansion.

> Same again – well done.

what always happens and when lives are lost talent is lost and families are destroyed. World War I is a classic example of this, when millions of young men were killed leaving millions of children and widows who then had to cope without the men.

Another drawback of going to war is when to stop. The war has to have clear aims. The UN demands that there are clear aims and some Just War Theories demand this too, but the problem here is that sometimes the aims are fine at the start but change as the war progresses. The aims of the Iraq war were fine at the start but, once they could not find WMDs, the aims seemed to change from WMD elimination to the elimination of Saddam Hussein and that is when people began to ask questions. That is also why there is still trouble in Iraq because Iraqi people can still sometimes view the invasion as an uninvited leadership change.

> Stating the drawback – good.

> Example from real life.

> And a practical example of how it can work out – excellent stuff.

High fives for this candidate. (I just put in 'high fives' to be cool, you understand.) This answer has everything that it needs to be worth full marks.

The Bad

Drawbacks of going to war are that people are killed. Civilians get killed and so do soldiers. Buildings are destroyed and it costs a lot to rebuild them. Transport and power is part of this and it has to be rebuilt too after the war on both sides and somebody has to pay.

> A point for the drawback and its explanation.

> Another point for this.

Not a good answer. There is little sign here that the candidate tried to learn any of this stuff – they could have walked in off the street and done it – hence two marks.

The Ugly

War has many drawbacks:

Cost

Death

Rebuilding —————————————

Revenge attacks

Harm to the environment

Suffering

> All correct – none explained – no marks.

This is a list. At Higher, this gets no marks.

# WORLD RELIGIONS: BUDDHISM

**Intermediate 2**

> State **two** ways a Buddhist might 'control his senses'. **2 KU**
> (2) (Int 2 Question (a) 2010)

The Good

A Buddhist might control his senses through meditation. Meditation involves concentration which allows Buddhists to control their physical senses. Following some steps of the Eightfold Path might be a help too. Right concentration might control senses because it is linked to meditation.

> Good start – straight into the answer, no messing about.

> Looks promising but more information is needed.

> Excellent follow-up just to make sure that the marker knows that you know what you are talking about.

**Brief and to the point with good expansion. An excellent no-nonsense answer.**

> Well done, we have further expansion. An easy two marks.

The Bad

The Eightfold Path will help Buddhists to meditate because the last three steps are about meditation. People control their senses through meditation.

> A promising start, now do something with it.

> Good point, but is that it? You need another point here to make sure of the two.

An opportunity missed here. The candidate clearly knows the answer but simply has not given enough. Silly and expensive error.

The Ugly

Buddhists control their senses by trying very hard to do it.

> You havin' a laugh? One or two years' study and this is all you can write?

This is the sort of answer that can cause RE teachers to sit and stare into space wondering, 'Why?'

---

What is meant by 'lower passions'?

**2KU**
(Int 2 Question (b) 2010)

---

The Good

Lower passions cause bad kamma. Lower passions are when Buddhists want things like money or possessions. They are attached to things that are not spiritual and will not help them achieve nibbana. A Buddhist would have the Three Poisons in their lower passions because they are about greed and hatred and ignorance. The greed is greed for material things and the hatred is doing harm to things and the ignorance is how they are ignorant of what life is really all about and they make the lower passions very strong. The Buddha said that the Middle Path was the way to overcome the lower passions because it helped to control the senses.

> Good start – you know what they are.

> Good point.

> Now you're giving examples although you haven't done anything with your kamma information.

> Yip, you've bagged the two marks.

> Like I said, you've bagged the two marks,

> Hello? You're writing too much – this is worth two marks!

This answer easily gets two marks but it is too long and this can cost time in the exam. Always check the value of a question and make sure you do not write too much, especially for low value questions.

## The Bad

Lower passions are the opposite of higher passions. Lower passions are things like greed and hatred. Lower passions stop Buddhists from achieving nibbana

> Is that a fact? No marks for this smart Alec.

> Good. You have said what they are.

**A weak answer. This candidate was struggling with the term 'lower passions'. There's a bit of guesswork going on here.**

> Bad – you are asked what is meant by lower passions not what they do.

## The Ugly

Lower passions are when Buddhists feel bad about stuff.

> Eh?

**No comment!**

---

Explain how a Buddhist might overcome the lower passions.
Give reasons for your answer.                                **6 AE**

(Int 2 Question (c) 2010)

---

## The Good

They can be overcome mainly through meditation. What happens in meditation is that you are detached from the world of senses and, by being detached from them, you are controlling their effect on you. Mara is temptation. The Buddha was tempted with physical pleasures by Mara and he overcame them by being disciplined and meditating. In monasteries, monks are taught how to overcome the lower passions and I think being in a community with other monks could make it easier when everyone is trying to achieve the same control. In the monastery, monks can observe the Five Precepts which help to

> Setting up the AE point nicely.

> Nailed it – two secure marks.

> Setting up AE again.

> And another excellent AE point to follow.

> Good follow-on point that gets you ready for the next AE point.

> Followed up superbly with yet another AE point.

cultivate detachment which is needed to control the lower passions.

> And brilliantly rounded off by taking the monks' point a further step.

First-rate answer. Each AE point is supported with evidence and that is exactly how you secure six marks in questions like this.

## The Bad

The lower passions are things like greed, desire and hatred. They are represented by the pig, the cockerel and the snake. Buddhists have to overcome these poisons to be able to achieve nibbana. The Buddha was tempted with these things by Mara, but he resisted and overcame the human condition. Meditation is the best way to overcome the lower passions because it teaches you how to detach yourself from the world. The dharma can also help because it has teachings on how to deal with the poisons that make the lower passions.

> This is all description. It is an AE question!

> Good recovery, back on AE track with this point.

> And with this point too but what a waste of time with the KU at the start.

The big problem with this answer is that most of it is taken up with KU. It is an AE question for goodness' sake. It is only when it starts talking about meditation that the marks start to flow. Take care to avoid doing this. It is a mistake that is frequently made.

## The Ugly

Buddhists overcome the passions by meditating. This helps them to control their desires which cause the lower passion.

> Teeing up your AE well here.

> And hitting the target but there's not enough in this answer!

Too brief. More examples and more information. You cannot realistically expect to get six marks for writing two lines. Think about it.

**Higher**

> In what ways do Buddhists meditate?                **6 KU**
>
>                                    (Higher Question (f) 2010)

## The Good

There are two types of meditation in Buddhism. One is Vipassana which is sometimes called insight meditation. This means concentrating on the thoughts that go on inside your head. In Therevada, Buddhism monks meditate on the Four Noble Truths and the Three Marks of Existence. In Mahayana, they meditate on the concept of sunyata and can also meditate on images of higher beings. Another type of meditation is samatha which is about exercises designed to calm each person and destroy mental distractions. People can use whatever pose they want for meditation. The important thing is control of breath, physical sensations and thoughts. This is done by focusing attention on an image, a shape, words or sounds.

*You sure about that? If you're not sure about something you should write things like, 'Buddhist meditation includes'.*

*Good point.*

*And followed up with expansion of the fact.*

*Yet more depth shown here – excellent technique.*

*More expansion of the first point, which shows a depth of knowledge – this is impressive.*

*Signs of struggle now but still enough in here for a mark.*

*Final two sentences get back on a bit more track and score points.*

This is the kind of answer that is seen quite often. Candidates start really well and go into a bit of detail before starting to struggle. However, very often if you know enough you will be able to grind out a few more marks even with general descriptions.

*It's a bit general but there's enough here to get a mark.*

## The Bad

Metta bhavana is very popular. It is about love meditation. You start off by feeling love for yourself, then your friends, then someone you are not wild about, then some you cannot stand and then you think

*OK, decent start. Now what are you going to do?*

about everyone around you who falls into these groups. You can also do vipassana and samatha.

> OK, you have given a good description of metta bhavana but the question asked for ways in which Buddhists meditate and you have only described one and named two. The most you'll get for this answer is three marks.

This answer contains the classic error that many candidates make. Where more than one thing is wanted they write loads about one thing and barely mention the other. Chances are that, if you do this, the most you could get is half marks for the question. Check to see if there are plurals such as 'methods', 'ways', 'reasons', 'approaches'.

## The Ugly

To meditate Buddhists sit for hours thinking about nothing. They have to go to a monastery to meditate and they must give up everything when they go to the monastery. Only monks can meditate properly. Meta Bhavana is meditation where you have to share the love with people.

> Eh, no!

> Possible mark here but you show little understanding of how meditation works.

> Who? And in any case you're wrong. Have you never watched 'Little Buddha'?

> OK, a mark here even if you have borrowed the phrase from Bebo.

This answer is very vague. The information in it is the kind that you might pick up if you have looked at various unrelated clips about Buddhism on Youtube as part of your intensive study programme. Falls well short of Higher standard.

---

'Living a moral life is more important than meditating.'    **8 AE**

Explain at least **two** ways in which Buddhists might respond to this statement.

(Higher Question (h) 2010)

---

## The Good

Living a moral life is just as important as meditating because all meditation techniques have morals. Mahayana Buddhists have sila which is made up of right speech, right

> Good start, one mark on the board.

conduct and right livelihood. All of these include moral rules. For example right speech means not saying anything that is bad or untrue. In the Eightfold Path morals are very important too because they are part of the path that leads to enlightenment which is gained through meditation. Some people might say that kamma is important too because it means that you have to be a good person. Living a good life is very important to lay Buddhists in Mahayana because they may not be able to attain enlightenment through meditation.

> Good point but it needs expansion.

> Well explained and it backs up your point.

> This doesn't really go anywhere.

> Good stuff but needs a bit of expansion to improve the quality. Worth a mark though.

Therevada Buddhists might disagree because the monks spend so much time in meditation. Almost half of the steps in the Eightfold Path are about meditation and an arhat spends time detaching himself from the world and the kamma that is in it. They say that to achieve enlightenment the Buddha had to meditate. Only he had to do more than simply be good. He had to focus his mind and think deeply rather than go out and do good things. They are not allowed to do bad things. It is important that they do not but the most important thing is that they meditate properly.

> Good point, now expand on it.

> Done it! Well done!

> Really important that this has been done. Questions asked for two ways and two ways have been clearly given.

> Good point – now back it up!

> Hmm, the answer fades here but the marks are in the bag so it's not a problem.

> Back-up provided.

**This candidate clearly refers to two ways and it names them. This is always a good tactic because if you make your answer too general you will give the impression that you do not really know two ways.**

## The Bad

A moral life is very important to Buddhism because it is in the Eightfold Path. Meditation is part of the Eightfold Path too so it is just as important because if it was not important, then it would not be in the path. Kamma also

> Good start.

> Good reasoning but you don't back it up!

shows that skilful actions are important for being a better person, but the Buddha achieved enlightenment by meditating so that shows it is equally important.

This is the classic nearly good answer. The right ideas have been identified **but** not once were the points expanded. Result? This could easily have scored eight marks but because none of the points were explained it is borderline. A disaster because the candidate clearly knew his or her stuff.

## The Ugly

Morals are very important to Buddhists because they have to be moral before they can meditate. Meditation comes in two forms which are vipassana and samatha. Lay people find meditation difficult but arhats can do it because they are full-time Buddhists. Lay people have to do good kamma so they will come back as something better in the next life. Morals are more important because they give a person good kamma and, if kamma is bad, there is no way enlightenment can be attained even if you do meditate. The Five Precepts are morals that Buddhists have and they can be quite hard to follow if you are not a monk. So yes, moral living is much more important than meditation.

> Promising start.

> Where's this going – maybe we're about to get some acute insights

> Fair enough but what has this to do with the question?

> Oh no, we're on the 'Everything I know About Buddhism' tour. Got to hunt for marks now.

> Aha, a mark, hard to find but a perfectly good point.

> Irrelevant.

> Where did this come from? Nothing in the answer that built up to this.

This candidate looks as though she did not know anything much about the topic. Let's say that she didn't and that what she has done is try to cobble something together to salvage a few marks rather than miss the question out altogether. Well, the gamble paid off because this is worth a couple of marks. So the moral of the story is … even though the bulk of this answer was gibberish there were a couple of nuggets of information that saved it from being a zero.

# WORLD RELIGIONS: CHRISTIANITY

**Intermediate 2**

> Explain why following the example of Jesus is important for Christians.
>
> **4 KU**
>
> (Int 2 Question (b) 2009)

The Good

Following the example of Jesus is important to Christians because:

1. He is God's son and through his life and teaching he showed people what God expected of them.
2. Jesus wanted people to be like him in order that more people would accept his teachings and turn to God.
3. Following Jesus' example will make you a better person and bring you closer to God.

> Each point gets a mark.

**Brief and to the point with good expansion, but it is worth four marks – worthwhile putting in a fourth point to make the last mark safe.**

The Bad

You should follow Jesus' example because it will make you a better person and that is important because you will be setting an example for other people.

> Really only one point made here.

**You're not going to get four marks for one point!**

The Ugly

Jesus set an example by healing the sick. He spoke to women as equals which was unusual in his time. He mixed with people who were hated by others like tax collectors and Romans.

> The question asks why it is important – all you have done is describe what Jesus did.

He ignored the Devil when he went into the desert. These are all examples of how Jesus set an example.

**In short – answer the question!**

> 'Belief in the resurrection should affect the way Christians live.'
> Would all Christians agree? Explain your answer fully.   8 AE
>
> (Int 2 Question (g) 2009)

The Good

The resurrection is a central belief of Christianity so it will have an affect on the way Christians live their lives. By believing in the resurrection, Christians are accepting that they are part of the Kingdom of God. The Kingdom of God has certain rules and standards of behaviour so, in that way, belief in the Resurrection will affect the way they live their lives

> Point well made, two marks.

It will affect their lives in other ways too. When a person dies they will, maybe, not be as sad because they believe in life after death and are therefore more sure that death is not the end.

> OK, not a bad point. Possibly worth two but certainly one.

It might also affect the way they live their lives because, on the cross, Jesus forgave the people who were killing him so, if Jesus can forgive people on the cross, then Christians should be able to forgive people in their daily lives.

> OK, fair point – worth a couple.

Also Jesus suffered on the cross to bring about good so, in the same way, we should be prepared to take on suffering to bring about good; so yes Christians agree that belief in it should affect the way they live their lives.

> Not sure about this one – probably not worth anything – just rounding off the answer.

This is a good answer but not out of the top drawer. Probably worth around 6 marks. The points could have been made a bit better.

## The Bad

Christians would totally agree with this statement. Very few Christians would disagree with it. Most Christians would think that it does affect the way they live their lives. Jesus showed that death is not the end and so we do not need to fear death and that means that we will not be scared of it. The resurrection shows Christians that they have to live a life where they believe that God loves them and wants them to forgive their enemies so yes I think Christians would agree with the question.

> Nothing is really said here and the same thing is said three times!

> Probably worth a couple of marks.

> And so too is this.

A weak answer. The candidate waffles a bit at the start and then gets to grips with the question. Half marks at best.

## The Ugly

The resurrection is when Jesus came back from the dead. He was put on trial and lost his case and was put to death. He forgave people on the cross. He was buried in the tomb and on the third day angels rolled away the stone and Jesus had come back from the dead. He met women who told the disciples he was back from the dead, but Thomas did not believe them. He met the disciples in several places and proved it was him by the way he broke the bread. This will affect the way Christians live their lives because it is true.

> This does not make any attempt to answer the question.

One comment – read the question!

**Higher**

> Describe the suffering and death of Jesus. **5 KU**
>
> (Higher Question 2 (a) 2008)

## The Good

The suffering of Jesus began when Judas decided to grass him up to the Jewish authorities. They got him arrested and after putting him on trial passed him onto the Romans and this is when things got really bad. Pilate could find no fault with him and so had him flogged and then the soldiers mocked him by placing a very painful crown of thorns on his head. The crowd decided that Jesus should die rather than a well known criminal, which was harsh. He was made to carry his cross to Calvary, but on the way he was helped by Simon. Once there he was crucified which is very gruesome and painful. One of the Gospels says he got a spear thrust into his side to hasten his death as he suffered in all the heat and eventually died.

> Finally, getting into the question! A mark.

> A mark for each of the points here.

This is an easy question and it is easy to pick up marks as you can see.

## The Bad

Jesus suffered on the cross when they banged big heavy nails into his hands and feet. He did not die straight away. It took a few hours and when he did die he said that it was done and the curtain in the Temple was torn in two.

> A mark for this but there's not really anything else worth a mark

An opportunity missed. This is an easy question and the candidate only writes about the crucifixion. Poor.

## The Ugly

*Jesus was crucified. This is when they hammer nails into you. After he was crucified he came back from the dead after three days when the women found him. They had seen him being lashed by the Romans with a whip thing.*

> Does not really get to grips with the question. A mark for vaguely writing about his suffering.

Very poor. The candidate does not even seem to know the story of the crucifixion.

---

Assess the importance of the suffering and death of Jesus as a means of salvation.

**10 AE**

(Higher question 2 (b) 2008)

---

## The Good

*The suffering and death of Jesus is hugely important for Christians aiming for salvation. The first point is that, without the suffering and death of Jesus, there can be no salvation. Various scholars, such as Calvin and Knox, have made a strong case for this, saying that belief in Jesus' death and resurrection is vital if a person wants to achieve salvation. It is called 'justification by faith' which means that you must have faith in Jesus' suffering and death as being for our salvation.*

> Good start – teeing up the AE point here.

> And then hitting us with two excellent points using sources. Worth at least a couple of marks.

*The second point is what Jesus' suffering and death actually achieved. The apostle Paul tells us that Jesus' death and suffering was God sending down his own son in order that our*

> Teeing up again.

> And then following up with three high quality points, each of which gets a mark.

relationship with him could be put right. God and humans were alienated (Adam, Eve and original sin explains how and why) and God needed a new covenant to help us get back on terms with him. This is what Jesus' death and suffering achieved. He died for our sins and, if we believe in this, we can bridge the gap with God. The final point is that, through the sacrifice of Jesus, God has shown humanity that he loves it. All that God requires in return is that humanity loves him back and accepts Jesus as its saviour. Christians often talk about Jesus 'saving us' and by this they mean that Jesus saves us from the consequences of our sin. The consequences are that we would be forever cast into hell but, because of his suffering and death, Jesus has given us the chance to avoid this simply by accepting him and having the faith that his sacrifice will lead us away from eternal damnation to salvation which is being with God for the rest of time when we die.

> Teeing up yet again.

> And yet again making three excellent points.

Excellent answer. The skill of teeing up points and then supporting them has made this an answer that would get at least eight marks, probably more. The length is about right and the use of sources is commendable

### The Bad

Jesus' suffering and death is very important. To get to heaven you have to believe in Jesus and what he did, so it is important in that way. It is also important because if there was no death and suffering of Jesus, then there would be no salvation and we would all go to Hell. Another thing is that we need to believe

> This is not bad. Three points have been made but they have not really been backed up with much explanation so it is worth only three marks.

in the suffering and death of Jesus to get to Heaven.

Some Christians say that it is important to believe in other things and do other things too. The suffering of Jesus is important, but it is also important that Christians help other people because that is what Jesus did and that will be important when God judges your life before you get into heaven. Overall though the importance is very true because it plays such an important part in things like Christian worship; Easter is a time when Christians think a lot about Jesus' suffering.

> Worth a mark because you are giving the alternative view.

> Bit too vague to be worth anything.

Not a great effort even though some good points have been made. The whole answer lacks explanations, which means it lacks depth.

### The Ugly

Salvation is important to Christians because it means that they can get into Heaven and meet up with relatives and friends again. It is important because Christians have to believe in it as part of their faith. Their belief in it would be pointless if there was no salvation.

> Waffle. Nothing of any note is said here.

How can I put this? Mince ... no, it is worse than that because mince can be quite nice – this isn't!

## TRY THIS

Let's give you some practice at building up good KU and AE answers. The KU questions are worth four marks. The level of exam is unimportant – it is the technique that we are after and in both exams the technique is the same. What you should do when you have done this is take any topic you have studied and break it down in the same way.

# Knowledge and Understanding

1. Describe the scientific method.                    **4 KU**
Now write your answer in the following way:

- Describe what observation is.
- Describe what a hypothesis is.
- Describe what an experiment is.
- Describe what verification is.
- Give an example of how it works in real life.

2. What evidence is there to support the Big Bang theory?  **4 KU**
Now write your answer in the following way:

- In one sentence say what the Big Bang is.
- Describe one piece of evidence you have learned.
- Give one sentence of explanation.
- Describe another piece of evidence you have learned.
- Give one sentence of explanation.
- Describe another piece of evidence you have learned.
- Give one sentence of explanation.
- Describe another piece of evidence you have learned.
- Give one sentence of explanation.

3. What are the main ideas of evolutionary theory?    **4 KU**
Now write your answer in the following way:

- Bullet point natural selection.
- After the bullet point explain what it is.
- Bullet point another idea.
- After the bullet point explain what it is.
- Bullet point another idea.
- After the bullet point explain what it is.
- Bullet point another idea.
- After the bullet point explain what it is.

## Analysis and Evaluation

1. 'Science is more reliable than revelation.'
To what extent is this statement justified?                **8 AE**

- Before you do anything, write in your own words what you think the statement is saying.
- Begin your answer by writing 'This statement is saying …' and then go on to explain what it says.
- Make a comment about how fair the statement is.
- Explain the comment you have made.
- Provide evidence or argument to back up the comment you have made.
- Refer back to the statement.
- Pick out one weakness of the comment.
- Refer back to the statement.
- Pick out one strength of the comment.
- Refer back to the statement.
- Make another statement and repeat the process another two times (including this one).
- Refer back to the statement.

2. 'Science provides a perfectly reasonable explanation as to the origins of the universe.'
Why might there be disagreement amongst Christians over this statement?                **8 AE**

- Before you do anything, write in your own words what you think the statement is saying.
- Begin your answer by writing 'This statement is saying …' and then go on to explain what it says.
- Make a comment about why there would be disagreement amongst Christians.
- Explain the comment you have made.
- Refer back to the statement.
- Make a comment about how one group of Christians would react.
- Provide evidence or argument to back up the comment you have made.

- Refer back to the statement.
- Repeat the previous two steps another two times.
- Refer back to the statement.

> 3. Do all Christians think it is possible to believe in both evolutionary theory and God at the same time?　　**8 AE**

- Before you do anything, write in your own words what you think the question is trying to get you to write about.
- Make a comment about the question and begin it thus: 'All Christians do not think it is possible to believe in both ...' etc.
- Explain the comment you have made.
- Make a comment about how one group of Christians would react.
- Refer back to the statement.
- Provide evidence or argument to back up the comment you have made.
- Refer back to the statement.
- Repeat the previous two steps another two times.
- Refer back to the statement.

# What is about to follow

*A brief explanation*

## A BRIEF EXPLANATION

We are now going to have a look at every section of the paper and how you can improve your AE performance in each section. Here is how I have set things out for you:

- There are two main sections. The first section is the question focus. These areas are the most popular or obvious focuses of questioning but they are **not** the only focuses of questioning; there could be others. I have made lists of the kinds of things you need to know, avoid and look out for.

- The second section has the heading 'Question approaches' and has examples of angles that questions might take. There are two bits of information here: questions and statements. The 'statements' is a selection of statements that might be used in the exam. In fact, I've made them a bit harder in some cases than the ones you will get in the exam because the purpose of this book is not just to get you a grade but to **boost** your grade. If you are able to deal with these statements then you'll be able to deal with most of the statements that are thrown at you in the exam

- When you are reading the statements remember that it is quite possible to put any of the concepts you have been learning about into the statement. Feel free to swap things around. In fact, many Higher RMPS classes have parties and do this kind of thing with their friends. Remember too to add on the questions that usually follow statements on the following pages.

- Those of you studying Intermediate 2 should have a copy of the SQA arrangements handy because I have provided information on the whole of the Higher course. The Int 2 course does not cover all the issues and concepts in the Higher course. Check the arrangements as you go along because some of the question areas will not apply to you.

- Every so often you will see 'Higher only' next to question approaches. This means that the topic in question does not appear at Int 2. That being said though, for most of the topics affected it is difficult to do the topic without including the 'Higher only' information. It would be a good idea to know the 'Higher only' topics if you are doing Int 2 since they will give you more to say about particular issues and topics.

- Finally, the book cannot cover every possible angle the exam can take. The ones listed are the ones that have been used most often. **Always** be prepared for questions that take new angles on issues.

# 4    Existence of God (Int 2 only)

*Area 1: The cosmological argument*

*Area 2: Design and purpose*

*Area 3: Evil and suffering*

## AREA 1: THE COSMOLOGICAL ARGUMENT

| Question Focus | Religious views on the origins of the universe |
|---|---|

*You need to know:*
- different religious views of how the universe began
- why Christians hold different views of the origins of the universe
- the ways in which Christians use the Bible/science to explain the origins of the universe
- reasons for Christian agreement/disagreement on the origins of the universe
- how Christians make the Big Bang theory fit into their beliefs
- why Christians see the Big Bang as proving the cosmological argument.

*You need to avoid:*
- giving the impression that all Christians believe the same about the origins of the universe
- mixing up different Christian views.

*You need to look out for:*
- questions that ask why Christians disagree about the way the universe was created
- questions that ask for where Christians agree on how the universe was created.

**Question approaches**

*Statements:*
- 'God created the universe as it is described in the Bible.'

- 'Science provides a perfectly reasonable explanation as to the origins of the universe.'
- 'God created the universe.'
- 'A literal understanding of the Genesis creation stories creates more problems than it solves.'

*Questions:*
- Why might some Christians disagree about how the universe was created?
- Explain the issues Christians agree upon in relation to the origins of the universe.
- Why do some Christians consider the Genesis creation story to be accurate?
- Does religion provide a satisfactory explanation for the origins of the universe?

| **Question Focus** | **Objections to Christian beliefs about the origin of the universe from science** |
|---|---|

*You need to know:*
- what scientific discoveries challenge Christian beliefs about the origin of the universe
- the objections to beliefs about the First Cause
- Christian responses to the objection
- reasons why some of the responses have worked or failed.

*You need to avoid:*
- giving the impression that all Christians believe the same about the origins of the universe
- mixing up different Christian views.

*You need to look out for:*
- questions that ask why Christians disagree about the way the universe was created
- questions that focus on one specific objection to a belief.

**Question approaches**

*Statements:*
- 'Science shows us that God did not create the universe.'
- 'Christians can believe in both the Big Bang theory and God at the same time.'
- 'The Big Bang theory proves that there is a First Cause.'
- 'The Big Bang theory disproves the Bible creation stories.'

- 'The Big Bang is God's way of creating.'
- 'Scientific theories concerning the origins of the universe leave no room for God.'

*Questions:*
- Why might some scientists think that Christian views about the origins of the universe are wrong?
- To what extent do you agree that scientific objections to God's involvement in creation are valid?
- How far do you agree that science offers nothing in the way of evidence to prove that God is the First Cause?
- How successfully do Christians respond to criticisms from science of their belief that God is the First Cause?

> **Question Focus** | **Conflict and co-operation between science and religion**

*You need to know:*
- areas where science and religion agree/disagree about the origins of the universe
- whether or not the two give complementary views of the origins of the universe
- reasons for agreement and disagreement
- reasons why both are needed to explain the origins of the universe.

*You need to avoid:*
- giving the impression that all Christians and all scientists believe the same about the origins of the universe
- mixing up different Christian and scientific views.

*You need to look out for:*
- questions that polarise (good word eh? Now go and look it up – you need a walk) science and religion
- questions that ask about agreement between science and religion
- questions that suggest some religious beliefs are no longer necessary.

**Question approaches**

*Statements:*
- 'Science and religion both contribute to our understanding of the origins of the universe.'
- 'Christians can accept both biblical and scientific views of the origins of the universe.'

- 'Science removes the need for a creator God.'
- 'Science can prove where the universe came from; religion cannot.'
- 'Nobody knows where the universe came from. It is all guesswork.'
- 'Christianity has nothing to fear from theories about the origins of the universe.'

*Questions:*
- To what extent can Christians and scientists agree on the origins of the universe?
- Why are science and religion sometimes opposed to each other on the issue of the origins of the universe?
- To what extent are both science and religion needed to explain the cause of the Universe?

# AREA 2: DESIGN AND PURPOSE

| Question Focus | Religious views on the origins of human life |
|---|---|

*You need to know:*
- different religious views of how life began
- why Christians hold different views of the origins of life
- the reasons for different Christian views on the origins of life
- whether or not Christians agree or disagree on the origins of life
- whether or not it is possible to be Christian and accept the findings of science
- how Christians make the evolutionary theory fit into their beliefs
- why Christians see evolutionary theory as proving the teleological argument.

*You need to avoid:*
- giving the impression that all Christians believe the same about the origins of life
- mixing up different Christian views.

*You need to look out for:*
- questions that ask why Christians disagree about the way life was created
- questions that ask for where Christians agree on how the universe was created.

**Question approaches**

*Statements:*
- 'God created human beings as it is described in the Bible.'

- 'Science provides a perfectly reasonable explanation as to the origins of the human life.'
- 'God created human life.'
- 'A literal understanding of the Genesis creation stories creates more problems than it solves.'

*Questions:*
- Why are the views of some Christians on the origins of life controversial?
- To what extent is interpretation of the Bible the key issue in the debate about human origins?
- Why is evolutionary theory considered by some to be an incomplete explanation of human origins?
- Is it reasonable to argue that, if evolution is true, then human existence is pointless?

**Question Focus**    **Challenges to beliefs about the origins of life**

*You need to know:*
- what scientific discoveries challenge Christian beliefs about the origin of life
- the challenge to beliefs about God and God as Designer
- Christian responses to each of the challenges
- reasons why some of the responses have worked or failed
- the challenges Christians pose each other.

*You need to avoid:*
- giving the impression that all Christians believe the same about the origins of the universe
- mixing up different Christian views.

*You need to look out for:*
- questions that ask why Christians disagree about the way that life was created
- questions that ask how successfully Christians respond to the challenges of science
- questions that focus on one specific challenge to a belief.

**Question approaches**

*Statements:*
- 'Christians can believe in both evolutionary theory and God at the same time.'
- 'Evolutionary theory proves that there is a God.'

- 'Evolutionary theory disproves the Bible creation stories.'
- 'Evolutionary theory shows that humans have no special purpose in nature.'
- 'Evolution is God's way of creating life.'
- 'If the evolutionary theory is right then either God does not exist or he is not what Christians imagine him to be.'

*Questions:*
- Explain why evolution might be a threat to some beliefs about God.
- To what extent is it possible to believe that a loving God created evolution?
- How far do Christians agree that evolution poses no threat to belief in God as Designer?
- Is it possible to argue for the existence of an all-knowing, all-powerful and all-loving God in the light of evolutionary theory?

# AREA 3: EVIL AND SUFFERING

| Question Focus | The challenge of natural and moral evil to beliefs about God |
| --- | --- |

*You need to know:*
- what natural and moral evil is
- the nature of God
- the problems caused by natural/moral evil for Christians
- Christian explanations for the existence of natural/moral evil.

*You need to avoid:*
- giving the impression that all Christians have the same response to natural/moral evil
- mixing up different Christian views.

*You need to look out for:*
- questions that ask why Christians might disagree about the extent of the challenges.

**Question approaches**

*Statements:*
- 'The greatest challenge to God's existence is natural evil.'
- 'In the light of the evil and suffering that exists in the world, God cannot be all powerful.'

- 'God created evil and suffering.'
- 'The suffering and evil in the world shows that God is a God of love.'

*Questions:*
- Why is moral evil a threat to Christian beliefs about God?
- To what extent does the existence of evil disprove the existence of God?
- How far would Christians agree that evil and suffering are necessary?
- Why is the existence of suffering and evil used to deny the existence of God by some people?

| Question Focus | Christians views on the origins of suffering |
|---|---|

*You need to know:*
- the story of the Fall
- the message of the story
- what original sin is
- the problems and answers the story provides for Christians on the issue of evil and suffering
- different interpretations of the story.

*You need to avoid:*
- giving the impression that all Christians believe the same about the Fall
- telling the whole story of creation.

*You need to look out for:*
- questions that ask why Christians disagree about the interpretation of the story
- questions that focus on a symbolic interpretation of the story
- questions that focus on one specific challenge to the story.

**Question approaches**

*Statements:*
- 'The story of the Fall should not be read literally.'
- 'The story of the Fall shows that humans are responsible for suffering and evil.'
- 'Suffering and evil are just part of existence; they have nothing to do with human disobedience.'
- 'The fact is that the possibility of suffering and evil was created by God so they are his responsibility.'

*Questions:*
- Explain why Christians disagree about the story of the Fall.
- Why might some people argue that God has some responsibility for suffering and evil?
- To what extent is the story of the Fall a reasonable explanation of the origins of suffering and evil?
- Explain why Christians believe that God allowed suffering and evil.

> | **Question Focus** | **The strengths, weaknesses and issues related to the free will defence** |
> | --- | --- |

*You need to know:*
- what the free will defence is
- different forms of the free will defence
- strengths/weaknesses of free will defence.

*You need to avoid:*
- giving the impression that there is only one form of the free will defence argument.

*You need to look out for:*
- questions that ask about one specific form of the free will defence
- questions that cut across different areas of this unit because this topic can easily do that.

**Question approaches**

*Statements:*
- 'Free will defence arguments have failed.'
- 'The free will defence argument is simply a lame excuse for God's failure to control suffering and evil.'
- 'Free will makes human existence meaningful.'
- 'God had no alternative but to create suffering and evil.'

*Questions:*
- To what extent is the free will defence successful?
- How does the free will defence work when it comes to explaining natural evil?
- Why is the free will defence necessary?
- If there was no free will what difference would it make to human existence?

# 5   Christianity: Belief and science

*Introduction*

*Area 1: Sources of understanding*

*Area 2: What is the origin of the universe?*

*Area 3: What is the origin of human life?*

## INTRODUCTION

This topic is covered at both Higher and Intermediate 2. If you are in a combined Higher-Int 2 class, you will all be studying this topic. The contents of Higher and Int 2 are very similar, with the main difference being that Higher goes into a bit more depth.

## AREA 1: SOURCES OF UNDERSTANDING

| Question Focus | Compare and contrast scientific method and revelation |
|---|---|

*You need to know:*
- what scientific method is
- what revelation is
- what they have in common
- what differences exist between them.

*You need to avoid:*
- portraying revelation as hapless superstition – take a balanced view
- portraying scientific method as flawless – scientists will not agree with that.

*You need to look out for:*
- questions that ask for the differences and similarities between the two
- questions that suggest both have their problems.

**Question approaches**

*Statements:*
- 'Science has a more reliable method of understanding the universe than revelation.'
- 'Revelation is no less reliable than scientific method in understanding the universe.'
- 'To understand the universe fully, both scientific method and revelation must be used.'

*Questions:*
- Compare and contrast scientific method with revelation.
- Explain the similarities between scientific method and revelation.
- Explain the differences between scientific method and religion.

| Question Focus | Strengths and weaknesses of scientific method |
|---|---|

*You need to know:*
- what scientific method is
- the ways in which scientific method can be seen to be strong/weak
- how science defends itself against its weaknesses
- whether the strengths outweigh the weaknesses.

*You need to avoid:*
- mixing up the strengths and weaknesses
- having too few strengths and weaknesses learned – this can be a big question so you will need lots of information and ideas.

*You need to look out for:*
- questions that ask how reliable science is
- questions that ask whether science is trusted too much.

**Question approaches**

*Statements:*
- 'Scientific method deals only with hard facts.'
- 'Science makes assumptions about the laws of the universe that it cannot support.'
- 'The main strength of scientific method is that it is neutral in its statements.'
- 'The weaknesses of scientific method are trivial.'

*Questions:*
- Explain two strengths of scientific method.
- Explain two weaknesses of scientific method.
- What problems does scientific method have in understanding the nature of reality?
- Why do some people consider scientific method to be flawed?
- How far can science be trusted to give an accurate understanding of the nature of reality?
- Explain why scientific method is considered by many to give an accurate view of the nature of reality.

| Question Focus | Strengths and weaknesses of revelation |
|---|---|

*You need to know:*
- what revelation is
- the ways in which revelation can be seen to be strong or weak
- how Christians defend revelation
- whether the strengths outweigh the weaknesses
- specific problems related to special revelation and general revelation.

*You need to avoid:*
- mixing up the strengths and weaknesses
- having too few strengths and weaknesses learned – this can be a big question so you will need lots of information and ideas.

*You need to look out for:*
- questions that ask how reliable revelation is
- questions that ask why revelation is criticised so often.

**Question approaches**

*Statements:*
- 'Revelation is based purely on faith, therefore it cannot be taken seriously.'
- 'It is the messages behind revelation that are important, not the stories related to it.'
- 'Literal understandings of revelation are indefensible.'
- 'Revelation is what makes Christianity seem out of touch with the modern world.'

*Questions:*
- Explain two strengths of revelation.
- What problems does revelation have in understanding the nature of reality?
- Why do some people consider revelation to be flawed?
- Why is revelation considered to be reliable by Christians?
- In what ways is revelation limited?
- Explain why revelation is considered by many to give an accurate view of nature of reality.

| Question Focus | Meaning and importance of revelation/scientific method |
|---|---|

*You need to know:*
- what scientific method is
- what revelation is
- why scientific method is important in understanding the universe
- how science sees the universe
- the meaning and purpose of revelation
- how Christians see the universe.

*You need to avoid:*
- missing this issue out – it's not covered so well in NABs and exams but it remains a key area.

*You need to look out for:*
- questions that ask about the meaning of revelation
- questions that ask about the importance of scientific method.

**Question approaches**

*Statements:*
- 'Revelation is essential to Christian belief today.'
- 'Revelation is an important method of understanding the purpose of the world.'
- 'Scientific method helps makes complete sense of why and how the world works.'
- 'Scientific method is all that we need to understand the universe.'

*Questions:*
- Explain the significance of revelation to Christians today.
- Why is scientific method so important to scientists?

- How important is it for Christians to accept revelation?
- Explain the meaning of revelation for Christians today.
- Explain the significance of scientific method.
- Comment on the importance of scientific method and revelation in understanding the nature of reality.

# AREA 2: WHAT IS THE ORIGIN OF THE UNIVERSE?

| Question Focus | Religious views on the origins of the universe |
|---|---|

*You need to know:*
- different religious views of how the universe began
- why Christians hold different views of the origins of the universe
- the ways in which Christians may use the Bible and science to explain the origins of the universe
- reasons for Christian agreement and disagreement on the origins of the universe
- whether or not it is possible to be Christian and accept the findings of science
- how Christians make the Big Bang theory fit into their beliefs
- why Christians see the Big Bang as proving the cosmological argument.

*You need to avoid:*
- giving the impression that all Christians believe the same about the origins of the universe
- mixing up different Christian views.

*You need to look out for:*
- questions that ask why Christians disagree about the way the universe was created
- questions that ask for where Christians agree on how the universe was created.

**Question approaches**

*Statements:*
- 'God created the universe as it is described in the Bible.'
- 'Science provides a perfectly reasonable explanation as to the origins of the universe.'
- 'God created the universe.'
- 'A literal understanding of the Genesis creation stories creates more problems than it solves.'

*Questions:*
- Why might some Christians disagree about how the universe was created?
- Explain the issues Christians agree upon in relation to the origins of the universe.
- Why do some Christians consider the Genesis creation story to be accurate?
- Does religion provide a satisfactory explanation for the origins of the universe?

| Question Focus | Challenges to Christian beliefs about the origin of the universe from science |
|---|---|

*You need to know:*
- what scientific discoveries challenge Christian beliefs about the origin of the universe
- the challenge to beliefs about God, the world, creation, the Bible and the First Cause
- Christian responses to each of the challenges
- reasons why some of the responses have worked or failed
- the challenges Christians pose each other.

*You need to avoid:*
- giving the impression that all Christians believe the same about the origins of the universe
- mixing up different Christian views.

*You need to look out for:*
- questions that ask why Christians disagree about the way the universe was created
- questions that ask how successfully Christians respond to the challenges of science
- questions that focus on one specific challenge to a belief.

**Question approaches**

*Statements:*
- 'Science shows us that God did not create the universe.'
- 'Christians can believe in both the Big Bang theory and God at the same time.'
- 'The Big Bang theory proves that there is a God.'
- 'The Big Bang theory disproves the Bible creation stories.'
- 'The Big Bang theory leaves our world without any purpose.'
- 'The Big Bang is God's way of creating.'

- 'Scientific theories concerning the origins of the universe leave no room for God.'
- 'It does not matter what science says about the origins of the universe; Earth still occupies a special place in the universe.'

*Questions:*
- Why might some scientists think that creationist Christian views about the origins of the universe are wrong?
- To what extent do you agree that scientific objections to God's involvement in creation are valid?
- How far do you agree that science offers nothing in the way of evidence to prove that God is the First Cause?
- How successfully do Christians respond to criticisms from science of their belief that God is the First Cause?

**Question Focus** | **Conflict and co-operation between science and religion**

*You need to know:*
- areas where science and religion agree and disagree about the origins of the universe
- whether or not the two give complementary views of the origins of the universe
- reasons for agreement and disagreement
- reasons why both are needed to explain the origins of the universe.

*You need to avoid:*
- giving the impression that all Christians and all scientists believe the same about the origins of the universe
- mixing up different Christian and scientific views.

*You need to look out for:*
- questions that polarise science and religion
- questions that ask about agreement between science and religion
- questions that suggest some religious beliefs are no longer necessary.

**Question approaches**

*Statements:*
- 'Science and religion both contribute to our understanding of the origins of the universe.'

- 'Christians can accept both biblical and scientific views of the origins of the universe.'
- 'Science removes the need for a creator God.'
- 'Science can never accept that a God is needed for creation.'
- 'Science can prove where the universe came from; religion cannot.'
- 'Nobody knows where the universe came from. It is all guesswork.'
- 'Christianity has nothing to fear from theories about the origins of the universe.'

*Questions:*
- To what extent can Christians and scientists agree on the origins of the universe?
- Why are science and religion sometimes opposed to each other on the issue of the origins of the universe?
- To what extent are both science and religion needed to explain the cause of the universe?

**Question Focus**    **Big Bang and cosmological argument (Higher only)**

*You need to know:*
- what the Big Bang theory is
- what the cosmological or First Cause argument is
- why the Big Bang theory might cause problems for or give help to the First Cause argument
- whether the Big Bang theory has anything to offer the First Cause argument in relation to its truth
- whether acceptance of the Big Bang theory means acceptance that there is a First Cause of the universe.

*You need to avoid:*
- confusing cosmological and teleological arguments
- thinking that the Big Bang is the cosmological argument – it isn't!
- thinking that the two have to be opposed – they need not be.

*You need to look out for:*
- questions that ask why Christians can accept the Big Bang theory and believe in God
- questions that focus on the problems caused by the Big Bang theory for the First Cause argument.

**Question approaches**

*Statements:*
- 'The Big Bang has finally disproved the cosmological argument.'
- 'The Big Bang theory proves that the cosmological argument is right.'
- 'The Big Bang theory and the cosmological argument have nothing to offer each other.'
- 'The cosmological argument proves that God is behind the Big Bang.'
- 'If a scientist accepts the Big Bang theory, then belief in a First Cause must surely follow.'
- 'The cosmological argument shows that it is impossible for the Big Bang to be the only explanation of the origins of the universe.'

*Questions:*
- Why might some people argue that the Big Bang theory disproves God?
- To what extent would Christians agree that the Big Bang theory supported Christian arguments for a First Cause?
- Why is the Big Bang theory considered a threat to the cosmological argument?
- To what extent have Christians successfully dealt with the threat of the Big Bang theory to their beliefs about the origins of the universe?

| Question Focus | Strengths and weaknesses of the cosmological argument (Higher only) |
| --- | --- |

*You need to know:*
- what the cosmological or First Cause argument is
- the conclusions drawn by the First Cause argument
- which conclusions attract the most criticism and support
- why some points of the First Cause argument are weak or strong
- how Christians deal with the weaknesses and strengths
- criticisms of defences of the strengths and weaknesses of the cosmological argument.

*You need to avoid:*
- mixing up cosmological and teleological
- mixing up strengths with weaknesses
- writing off the First Cause argument as very weak or promoting it as very strong.

*You need to look out for:*
- questions that include Aquinas' name
- opportunities to expand on the criticisms and responses. Make your point and then add a bit more to it – don't leave it hanging there.

**Question approaches**

*Statements:*
- 'The cosmological argument fails to prove the existence of God.'
- 'The cosmological argument proves beyond all doubt that God exists.'
- 'The cosmological argument proves there is a First Cause and nothing else.'

*Questions:*
- Does there need to be a First Cause?
- Why did Aquinas think that a First Cause was necessary?
- Does the universe need a First Cause?
- How convincing is the First Cause argument put forward by Aquinas?
- How can it be argued that the First Cause argument is wrong?

# AREA 3: WHAT IS THE ORIGIN OF HUMAN LIFE?

| **Question Focus** | **Religious views on the origins of human life** |
|---|---|

*You need to know:*
- different religious views of how life began
- why Christians hold different views of the origins of life
- the way in which some Christians use the Bible, science or both to explain its origins
- the reasons for different Christian views on the origins of life
- whether or not Christians agree or disagree on the origins of life
- whether or not it is possible to be Christian and accept the findings of science
- how Christians make the evolutionary theory fit into their beliefs
- why Christians see the evolutionary theory as proving the teleological argument.

*You need to avoid:*
- giving the impression that all Christians believe the same about the origins of life
- mixing up different Christian views.

*You need to look out for:*
- questions that ask why Christians disagree about the way life was created
- questions that ask for where Christians agree on how the universe was created.

## Question approaches

*Statements:*
- 'God created human beings as it is described in the Bible.'
- 'Science provides a perfectly reasonable explanation as to the origins of human life.'
- 'God created human life.'
- 'A literal understanding of the Genesis creation stories creates more problems than it solves.'

*Questions:*
- Why are the views of some Christians on the origins of life controversial?
- To what extent is interpretation of the Bible the key issue in the debate about human origins?
- Why is evolutionary theory considered by some to be an incomplete explanation of human origins?
- Is it reasonable to argue that, if evolution is true, then, human existence is pointless?

| Question Focus | Challenges to beliefs about the origins of life |
|---|---|

*You need to know:*
- which scientific discoveries challenge Christian beliefs about the origin of life
- the challenge to beliefs about God, human life, human purpose, creation, God as Designer, the Bible
- Christian responses to each of the challenges
- reasons why some of the responses have worked or failed
- the challenges Christians pose each other.

*You need to avoid:*
- giving the impression that all Christians believe the same about the origins of the universe
- mixing up different Christian views.

*You need to look out for:*
- questions that ask why Christians disagree about the way life was created

- questions that ask how successfully Christians respond to the challenges of science
- questions that focus on one specific challenge to a belief.

**Question approaches**

*Statements:*
- 'Evolutionary theory poses a major threat to Christian belief.'
- 'Christians can believe in both evolutionary theory and God at the same time.'
- 'Evolutionary theory disproves the Bible creation stories.'
- 'Evolutionary theory shows that humans have no special purpose in nature.'
- 'Evolution is God's way of creating life.'
- 'Christians who accept evolution must reject biblical creation stories.'
- 'If evolutionary theory is right, then either God does not exist or he is not what Christians imagine him to be.'

*Questions:*
- To what extent does evolutionary theory disprove the existence of God?
- How far would Christians agree that evolution shows God to be a cruel and wasteful creator?
- Why might evolutionary theory convince some Christians that humans are a special creation?
- Why do Christians disagree over the theory of evolution?

| Question Focus | Conflict and co-operation between science and religion |
|---|---|

*You need to know:*
- areas where science and religion agree and disagree about the origins of life
- whether or not the two give complementary views of the origins of life
- reasons for agreement and disagreement
- reasons why both are needed to explain the origins of life.

*You need to avoid:*
- giving the impression that all Christians and scientists believe the same about the origins of the universe
- mixing up different Christian and scientific views.

*You need to look out for:*
- questions that polarise science and religion. (Have you not looked up 'polarise' yet? Go and do it **now**!)

- questions that ask about agreement between science and religion
- questions that suggest some religious beliefs are no longer necessary.

**Question approaches**

*Statements:*
- 'Science and religion both contribute to our understanding of the origins of human life.'
- 'Christians can accept both biblical and scientific views of the origins of human life.'
- 'Evolutionary theory has stripped human beings of both design and purpose in the world.'
- 'Evolution alone cannot explain the complexity of life; God has to be included.'
- 'Evolution need not be a threat to Christian belief.'
- 'The biblical accounts of the origins of humans are historically accurate.'
- 'Christianity has nothing to fear from theories about the origins of human life.'

*Questions:*
- To what extent can scientists accept some teachings of Christianity on the origins of life?
- How far do Christians and scientists agree on the purpose of human life?
- Why do some people believe that both science and religion are needed to explain the origins of human life?
- Is it reasonable to argue that evolution can show that humans are indeed a special creation by God?

| Question Focus | Evolution and teleological argument (Higher only) |
| --- | --- |

*You need to know:*
- what evolutionary theory is
- what the teleological (design) argument is
- why evolutionary theory might cause problems for, or give help to, the design argument
- whether the evolutionary theory has anything to offer the teleological argument in relation to its truth
- whether acceptance of the evolutionary theory means acceptance that there is a designer of the universe.

*You need to avoid:*
- confusing cosmological and teleological arguments

- using the Big Bang theory as part of evolutionary theory
- thinking that the two have to be opposed – they need not be.

*You need to look out for:*
- questions that ask why Christians can accept evolutionary theory and believe in God
- questions that focus on the problems caused by evolutionary theory for the Design argument.

**Question approaches**

*Statements:*
- 'Evolutionary theory shows that the design argument has failed.'
- 'Evolution requires God to design it.'
- 'Complexity in nature points to design not evolution.'
- 'Evolution is simply God's way of designing the universe.'
- 'Evolution shows that the teleological argument is wishful thinking.'
- 'Evolutionary theory and the teleological argument are both required to explain the origin of human life.'
- 'The teleological argument has successfully overcome the threat posed by scientific explanations of the origin of life.'

*Questions:*
- Why do some people believe that evolution removes the need for a Designer of the universe?
- To what extent do you agree that evolution requires a Designer?
- How far do you agree that the most serious objection to the design argument comes from evolution?
- If evolution is true, what effect might it have on Christian beliefs about God?

| Question Focus | Strengths and weaknesses of the teleological argument (Higher only) |
|---|---|

*You need to know:*
- What the teleological or design argument is
- What conclusions attract the most criticism and support
- Why some points of the design argument are weak or strong
- How Christians deal with the weaknesses and strengths
- Criticisms of defences of the strengths and weaknesses of the design argument.

*You need to avoid:*
- mixing up cosmological and teleological
- mixing up strengths with weaknesses
- writing off the Design argument as very weak or promoting it as very strong.

*You need to look out for:*
- questions that include Paley's name
- opportunities to expand on the criticisms and responses. Make your point and then add a bit more to it – don't leave it hanging there.

## Question approaches

*Statements:*
- 'The design argument fails to prove the existence of God.'
- 'The teleological argument proves beyond all doubt that God exists.'
- 'The design argument proves nothing more than the possibility of a Designer.'
- 'We choose to see design where there is none. Everything is down to a combination of natural laws and chance.'

*Questions:*
- Is the universe designed?
- Why did Paley think that the universe required a Designer?
- Does the universe need a Designer?
- How convincing is the design argument put forward by Paley?
- How can it be argued that the teleological argument is wrong?

# 6 Morality in the modern world (the Higher-only bit)

*Knowledge and Understanding questions*

*The relationship between religion and moral values*

*Analysis and Evaluation questions*

*The relationship between religion and moral values*

If you are doing Intermediate 2 then go away – you are not welcome here. This chapter is for Higher students only and there are secrets in here that only they should know. There is an odd little section in Morality in the Modern World that is all too often not properly studied by candidates, which is a shame because this is probably the most predictable part of the paper and therefore an area where serious marks can be picked up.

Your teacher will have chosen the moral issue you will study. On top of that, there's a bit called 'The Relationship between Religion and Moral Values' – a catchy title if ever there was one. In ancient past papers, you will see that there were once two sections in the morality section. One covered the 'Relationship between etc.' and the other covered the actual moral issue you have been doing. This has changed and now they are together in one section. The 'Relationship' stuff is worth around 10 KU and 4 AE in the exam and in the NABs. The Specimen Question Paper (SQP) sets out how it appears in the Crime and Punishment section, for example:

---

1. (a) Describe the Euthyphro dilemma. **3 KU**

   (b) What is the role of sacred writings in religious
       morality? **4 KU**

   (c) Explain the main features of utilitarian ethics. **3 KU**

   (d) How might utilitarians respond to issues arising
       from capital punishment? **4 AE**

---

The question is the same in all the topics except that in question (d) the 'issues arising' will be from the topic you have studied. You will be asked to analyse **not** evaluate in this question.

# KNOWLEDGE AND UNDERSTANDING QUESTIONS

Two or three questions will be descriptive questions on the Euthyrho Dilemma, utilitarianism and Kantian ethics – it is almost guaranteed. This means that the marks here should be a straightforward process if you have learned your stuff. **Be warned – year after year the SQA reports that candidates do not do this area well. Study it hard, don't gloss over it because ten marks are there for the taking.**

# THE RELATIONSHIP BETWEEN RELIGION AND MORAL VALUES

| Question Focus | Description of the Euthyphro dilemma |
|---|---|

*You need to know:*
- what the Euthyphro dilemma is
- what issue the Euthyphro dilemma addresses
- the story of the Euthyphro dilemma
- who presented the story.

*You need to avoid:*
- simply telling the story if the question asks what issue the Euthyphro dilemma raises – marks for doing this, er, zilch!
- saying 'Euthyphro' to anyone sitting next to you because they will get covered in spit
- naming your first child Euthyphro, because everyone will ask what his dilemma is.

*You need to look out for:*
- questions that include the phrase 'what issues about morality' – this means you do not tell the story but write about the issues.

**Question approaches**
- What problems with morality does the Euthyphro dilemma highlight?
- What issue does the Euthyphro dilemma address?
- What issue relating to morality did Plato discuss in the Euthyphro dilemma?
- What is the Euthyphro dilemma?

- Give a description of the Euthyphro dilemma.
- What points about morality was the Euthyphro dilemma attempting to make?

> **Question Focus**   **Description of religious morality**

*You need to know:*
- different sources of religious morality
- how each source is used to work out responses to moral issues.

*You need to avoid:*
- saying that any particular religion's sacred book is the only source. This is not true, for all religions!
- being vague about the sources – they are clear: tradition, sacred books, spiritual influence, notable teachers, and human reason.

*You need to look out for:*
- questions that focus on one source of religious morality.

**Question approaches**

- What are the sources of religious morality?
- Describe the role of tradition as a source of moral guidance in one religion you have studied.
- Explain the importance of sacred writings in religious morality.
- What sources does religion use to develop its moral values?

> **Question Focus**   **Description of Kantian ethics**

*You need to know:*
- what the key principles of Kantian ethics are
- what the 'summum bonum' is
- what the 'categorical imperative' is
- what 'acting as a lawgiver' means
- what 'universalisation of a law' means
- what 'not using people solely as a means to an end' means.

*You need to avoid:*
- confusing Kant with utilitarianism
- focusing only on one aspect of Kant – do them all.

*You need to look out for:*
- questions that specify one aspect of Kantian ethics

- questions that ask about ethics based on reason and duty – it's Kant.

**Question approaches**

- What is the categorical imperative?
- What did Kant mean when he wrote of universalising an act?
- What is the role of duty in Kantian ethics?
- Describe Kant's approach to moral decision making.
- Describe an ethical approach that is based on reason and duty.

| Question Focus | Description of utilitarian ethics |
|---|---|

*You need to know:*

- about Mill and Bentham
- about act utilitarianism
- about rule utilitarianism
- the differences between the two
- that utilitarianism is consequentialist
- that utilitarianism is about basing decisions on the consequences of an act.

*You need to avoid:*

- getting act and rule mixed up
- confusing utilitarianism with Kantian ethics.

*You need to look out for:*

- questions that ask about one type of utilitarianism
- questions that ask for common features of the two.

**Question approaches**

- Describe act and rule utilitarianism.
- What approach to moral decision making did Bentham and Mill suggest?
- What are consequentialist ethics?
- What principles lie behind consequentialist ethics?
- Describe the differences between act and rule utilitarianism.

# ANALYSIS AND EVALUATION QUESTIONS

Of all the AE questions in the paper, it looks as though the Religion and Moral Values one is the most predictable. Looking at various papers, the wording is very similar, probably because the analysis you are being asked to do is pretty difficult, but it looks as though it is analysis that you can learn. Note that, in this question, there is no evaluation, which tends to be about giving your view on something or criticising something or other. This AE question just asks you to apply something, which is why it is analysis. Follow me? No? Well, if you are sitting comfortably I shall explain.

The SQA wants you to apply the moral principles you have learned to the two issues you have studied in your topic. So, if you have studied Medical Ethics then there will be a question asking you what some moral stance would say about issues arising from The Use of Embryos **or** Euthanasia. Your answer can be on any issue within these two topics. The PA's report has made this clear.

The question for this area is worded similarly in the NABs, in the SQP and in past papers, so there is a hidden message here from the SQA that this is how it will be done.

# THE RELATIONSHIP BETWEEN RELIGION AND MORAL VALUES

| Question Focus | Applying moral stances to moral issues |
| --- | --- |

*You need to know:*
- the Kantian view of the two moral issues you have studied
- the utilitarian view of the two moral issues you have studied
- religious views of the two moral issues you have studied.

*You need to avoid:*
- panicking when you see this question – it's a gift
- having a debate about Kantian, etc views in this answer. All you need to do is show that you can apply them to the general moral issues you have studied.

*You need to look out for:*
- questions like this every year – they are a certainty.

**Question approaches**
- What approach might utilitarians take to issues arising from ...?
- With reference to one religion you have studied, what views might it have on issues arising from ...?
- Explain Kantian responses to moral issues arising from ...

# 7    Morality in the modern world

**Causes of crime and purposes of punishment**

**Capital punishment**

## CAUSES OF CRIME AND PURPOSES OF PUNISHMENT

| Question Focus | Causes of crime as an explanation for crime |
|---|---|

*You need to know:*

- the link between crime and its causes
- why some people reject or accept these links
- why the causes of crime can be controversial
- four or five points about the causes of crime and related issues, to be safe.

*You need to avoid:*

- confusing the causes of crime and purposes of punishment. (This should be impossible, I know, but it has been done!)

*You need to look out for:*

- questions that ask you for a discussion of one particular cause. Make sure you can write in detail about at least three of the causes.

**Question approaches**

*Statements:*

- 'The causes of crime are simply excuses for unacceptable behaviour.'
- 'Every criminal has understandable reasons for committing crimes.'
- 'The causes of crime are a concern for everyone.'
- 'Behind every crime there is an individual who has been let down by society.'

*Questions:*

- Why should the causes of crime be a concern for religious people?
- To what extent is society to blame for crime, rather than the individual?
- How far do you agree that the causes of crime should be considered before deciding on punishment for criminals?

---

| **Question Focus** | **Effectiveness of dealing with causes of crime** |
| --- | --- |

*You need to know:*

- what has been done by religious and secular groups to help those affected by the causes of crime, e.g. religious groups' work with addicts, government initiatives in deprived areas, community police projects
- the successes and failures that have been experienced by these different initiatives.
- why some people feel that tackling the causes of crime is pointless
- why some feel that we have a duty to tackle the causes of crime.

*You need to avoid:*

- writing about the purposes of punishment – very easy to stray off into that topic here.

*You need to look out for:*

- questions that ask for information on this topic – they are probably the trickiest questions in this topic.

**Question approaches**

*Statements:*

- 'Religious responses to crime are weak and ineffective.'
- 'Responses to the causes of crime simply do not work.'
- 'Everyone has a responsibility to tackle the causes of crime.'
- 'The only effective response to the causes of crime is to get tough on criminals.'
- 'Responses to the causes of crime tend to be all talk and no action.'

*Questions:*

- How effective are religious responses to the causes of crime?
- To what extent are secular responses to the causes of crime successful?
- Do you agree that responses to the causes of crime have limited success?

| Question Focus | Causes of crime as a concern for religious/secular groups |
|---|---|

*You need to know:*
- what the religious and secular views are – you will find that they are very similar and it is a good thing to point this out
- why religious and secular groups are concerned about the causes of crime.

*You need to avoid:*
- thinking that it is only opinions that are wanted here; religious concerns can be shown by the responses they have.

*You need to look out for:*
- questions that ask for a religious view – your answer will contain loads of secular insights that are shared with religious people but you need to find a couple of things that are clearly religious.

**Question approaches**

*Statements:*
- 'We should concentrate on punishing criminals, not understanding why they commit crimes.'
- 'You cannot consider how to punish criminals without understanding why they committed their crimes.'
- 'The reasons behind someone committing a crime are more important than how we punish them.'
- 'When an individual commits a crime it is always his or her choice to do so.'
- 'Being poor or coming from a difficult background is no excuse for criminal behaviour.'
- 'To be truly forgiving, religious people should show great concern about the causes of crime.'

*Questions:*
- Why should the causes of crime be a concern?
- Why do some people consider criminals to be victims?
- To what extent should society be concerned about the causes of crime?
- How far do you agree that crime is down to individuals simply being greedy?
- Has religion got anything to contribute to the debate about the causes of crime?

| Question Focus | Benefits, difficulties, strengths and weaknesses of each purpose of punishment |
|---|---|

*You need to know:*
- the good and bad points of each purpose of punishment you have studied
- the successes and failures of each purpose of punishment
- why some people prefer one purpose, or combinations of purposes, over others
- examples of these benefits, etc. from real life.
- your own handcrafted examples, gleaned from the life full of retributive punishment you are currently experiencing at school.

*You need to avoid:*
- confusing retribution and reformation.

*You need to look out for:*
- questions that focus on one purpose – you need to have loads to write here
- questions that ask you to explain the success or failure of different purposes of punishment.

**Question approaches**

*Statements:*
- 'Retribution is the only effective purpose of punishment.'
- 'Protection is the top priority for any punishment.'
- 'Deterrence does not work because people still commit crimes.'
- 'Reformation is a soft option for criminals.'
- 'Criminals do not need to be reformed; they need to suffer for their crimes.'
- 'Society must be prepared to give criminals another chance in life.'

*Questions:*
- Why do some people argue that retribution is essential to punishment?
- Explain two weaknesses of protection as a purpose of punishment.
- To what extent does deterrence, as a purpose of punishment, benefit society?
- How far do you agree that reformation is a soft option for criminals?
- Explain three strengths of retribution as a purpose of punishment.
- Do you agree that the most important purpose of punishment is deterring others from committing the same crime?

> | **Question Focus** | **Purposes of punishment as a religious or secular concern for society** |

*You need to know:*
- what the religious and secular views are – you will find that they are very similar and it is a good thing to point this out
- why religious and secular groups are concerned about the purposes of punishment.

*You need to avoid:*
- confusing the different purposes of punishment.

*You need to look out for:*
- questions that ask for a religious view – your answer will contain loads of secular insights that are shared with religious people but you need to find a couple of things that are clearly religious
- questions that focus on one particular purpose of punishment and whether it could be justified by a religious person
- questions about religious and secular reasons for not using certain purposes of punishment.

**Question approaches**

*Statements:*
- 'Punishment should only be about reforming an individual.'
- 'Deterrence does not work because people still commit crimes.'
- 'Criminals should be forgiven for their crimes.'
- 'Punishment does not solve anything.'
- 'Punishment is not for revenge, but to lessen crime and reform the criminal.'

*Elizabeth Fry*

*Questions:*
- How far do you agree that the only purpose of punishment that is morally acceptable is reformation?
- Explain how retribution, as a purpose of punishment, can be supported from a secular point of view.
- Explain what purpose of punishment should give society the greatest cause for concern.

> | **Question Focus** | **Benefits, difficulties, strengths and weaknesses of different sentences in the UK** |

*You need to know:*
- the different sentences that are used
- the good and bad points about different sentences
- at least a couple in some depth, in case there is a focus on one sentence only.

*You need to avoid:*
- writing about capital punishment here – it is not a sentence handed down by UK courts.

*You need to look out for:*
- questions that focus on one particular sentence.

**Question approaches**

*Statements:*
- 'Community service is good for both society and the criminal.'
- 'Community service is so weak as a punishment, it is hardly worth having.'
- 'Imprisonment is seen by many as a soft option.'
- 'Life imprisonment should mean 'life'.'
- 'Fines are the most effective punishment because criminals suffer and the state gets money.'
- 'There is only one suitable punishment for any crime – imprisonment.'
- 'Religious people can support only punishments that show compassion.'
- 'Without forgiveness, criminals will never change.'
- 'Religions demands justice. Retribution as a purpose of punishment gives it.'

*Questions:*
- Why do some people argue that retribution is essential to punishment?
- Explain two weaknesses of protection as a purpose of punishment.
- To what extent does deterrence, as a purpose of punishment, benefit society?
- How far do you agree that reformation is a soft option for criminals?
- Explain three strengths of retribution as a purpose of punishment.
- Explain two benefits of imprisoning criminals.
- Why is community service sometimes considered to be an inadequate punishment?
- Why should the purposes of punishment be a concern for religious people?

---

| Question Focus | UK sentencing as a concern for society and religion |
|---|---|

*You need to know:*

- what the religious and secular views are – you will find that they are very similar and it is a good thing to point this out
- why religious and secular groups are concerned about the sentences handed down.

*You need to avoid:*

- discussing capital punishment, because it is not a punishment that is handed down in the UK.

*You need to look out for:*

- questions that ask for a religious view – your answer will contain loads of secular insights that are shared with religious people but you need to find a couple of things that are clearly religious
- questions that focus on one particular sentence and whether it could be justified by a religious person
- questions about religious and secular reasons for not using certain sentences.

**Question approaches**

*Statements:*

- 'Community service is good for both society and the criminal.'
- 'Community service is so weak as a punishment, it is hardly worth having.'
- 'Imprisonment is seen by many as a soft option.'
- 'Fines are the most effective punishment because criminals suffer and the state gets money.'
- 'There is only one suitable punishment for any crime – imprisonment.'
- 'The first priority of the justice system is to protect the public from criminals.'

*Questions:*

- Why do some religious people argue that retribution is essential to punishment?
- Why do some people consider community service a weak response to crime?
- Explain why sentencing should be a concern of religion.
- Explain the views of one secular response to imprisonment you have studied.
- Do you agree that the most important purpose of punishment is deterring others from committing the same crime?

# CAPITAL PUNISHMENT

**Question Focus** | **Effectiveness of capital punishment**

*You need to know:*
- why capital punishment is seen as effective or ineffective.

*You need to avoid:*
- getting hooked on just one or two reasons for its effectiveness – there are many reasons for its effectiveness and ineffectiveness, but very often candidates end up just writing loads about one.

*You need to look out for:*
- questions that link capital punishment to the purposes of punishment
- questions that focus on one particular aspect of capital punishment.

**Question approaches**

*Statements:*
- 'To take a life when a life has been lost is revenge, not justice.'

*Desmond Tutu*
- 'Taking your life when you have taken the life of another – now that is true justice!'
- 'There is no evidence that the death penalty reduces crime.'
- 'The death penalty removes the problem; it does not solve it.'
- 'The death penalty works only for those who want revenge.'
- 'If the death penalty was a real deterrent, then nobody would commit crimes that could result in it.'

*Questions:*
- Why do some people consider the death penalty to be effective?
- To what extent is the death penalty successful as a deterrent?
- How far do you agree with the view that the death penalty is effective only as a form of revenge?
- Explain the advantages of having the death penalty.
- Why are there concerns about the death penalty?

| Question Focus | Strengths and weaknesses of arguments for and against capital punishment |
|---|---|

*You need to know:*
- the arguments for and against capital punishment
- at least three weaknesses and strengths of each argument.

*You need to avoid:*
- getting hooked on one strength or weakness when you are asked for more in the question. It often happens that candidates cannot get themselves off the strength or weakness they are on.

*You need to look out for:*
- questions that ask for an opinion about strengths outweighing weaknesses or something similar – take a safe middle line.

**Question approaches**

*Statements:*
- 'Regardless of the method, the death penalty can never be right.'
- 'The death penalty shows that human life is sacred.'
- 'The death penalty is more compassionate than life imprisonment.'
- 'The loss of one innocent life to execution is a price worth paying.'
- 'If killing is wrong, it is wrong in all cases and for all reasons.'
- 'The death penalty violates human rights, in a ruthless, absolute and irreversible manner.'
- 'Killing is wrong. It makes no sense that we kill murderers to show them that killing is wrong.'

*Questions:*
- Explain two strengths of the arguments against the death penalty.
- Why do some people consider capital punishment to be inhuman?
- Giving reasons for your answer, explain why some people consider executions to be humane.
- To what extent do you agree that the death penalty can never be right?
- Evaluate two arguments that support the death penalty.
- How important are human rights in the debate about capital punishment?

| Question Focus | Effectiveness of UN Declarations |
|---|---|

*You need to know:*
- what the Conventions are
- at least three criticisms and supporting views of each Declaration or Convention you have studied.
- what themes run through the Declarations and related Conventions.
- the effectiveness of the Declarations and related Conventions.

*You need to avoid:*
- confusing the various Conventions.

*You need to look out for:*
- questions that focus on the themes running through the Conventions, because they are looking for an overview
- questions that focus on the success of the Conventions – take a middle line here.

**Question approaches**

*Statements:*
- 'The UN Declarations have little or no effect on countries who use the death penalty.'
- 'The UN Declaration on the Right to Life is routinely ignored by countries using the death penalty.'
- 'Until the UN declares that the death penalty is wrong, innocent people will continue to be executed by member states.'
- 'The UN's position on capital punishment is confusing and unclear.'

*Questions:*
- To what extent does the UN support the death penalty?
- Why is the UN position on capital punishment criticised by some nations?
- How effective are UN Declarations in discouraging countries from using capital punishment?
- Assess the effectiveness of UN Declarations relating to capital punishment.

> **Question Focus**    **Evaluation of religious and secular views on capital punishment**

*You need to know:*
- what the religious and secular views are – you will find that they are very similar and it is a good thing to point this out.
- why religious and secular groups are concerned about capital punishment.

*You need to avoid:*
- generalising religious views – there are many shades of opinion.

*You need to look out for:*
- questions that ask for a religious view – your answer will contain loads of secular insights that are shared with religious people but you need to find a couple of things that are clearly religious
- questions that focus on one particular reason for having the death penalty and whether it could be justified by a religious person
- questions about religious and secular reasons for not using the death penalty.

**Question approaches**

*Statements:*
- 'Religious people cannot support capital punishment.'
- 'By murdering, a murderer is showing that he or she no longer considers life as sacred. For that reason he or she should be executed.'
- 'The only way to deter murderers is to have the death penalty.'
- 'Any action that causes harm to another individual is morally wrong.'

*Questions:*
- Explain the strengths and weaknesses of at least one religious argument used in the debate about capital punishment.
- Explain the strengths of at least one secular argument used in the debate about capital punishment.
- Explain the objections that some people might have to one religious view of capital punishment that you have studied.
- On what grounds might one secular view of capital punishment that you have studied be criticised?
- Discuss the support that can be provided for one religious position on capital punishment.

# 8 Morality in the modern world – Global issues

*Global distribution of wealth and resources*

*Global warming*

## GLOBAL DISTRIBUTION OF WEALTH AND RESOURCES

**Question Focus**

Evaluate religious and secular views or concerns on the distribution of wealth and resources, debt cancellation (Higher only), poverty, trading inequalities, political change and natural disasters

*You need to know:*

- what the problems and issues are of each area
- who is to blame for the problems arising from these issues
- the moral problems arising from each of the areas
- religious and secular views of the concerns.

*You need to avoid:*

- focusing on only one issue – you could be asked about all or any one of them.
- sweeping generalisations and exaggerations to make a point – the facts are brutal enough.

*You need to look out for:*

- questions that ask you to comment on religious and secular responses
- questions that look for you to assess how accurate religious or secular views are
- questions that ask you whether religious or secular responses are better.

## Question approaches

*Statements:*

- 'The biggest challenge in tackling poverty is removing trading inequality.'
- 'Without debt cancellation, poverty will never be removed.'
- 'The current distribution of wealth and resources breaks every moral rule in the book.'
- 'The economic problems of the poor are so great that they will never be solved.'
- 'The best solution to the problems poor countries face is political stability'.
- 'The blame for poverty lies mainly with rich countries.'
- 'Religion does little to help tackle the causes of poverty.'
- 'Religious responses to the global distribution of wealth and resources change nothing.'

*Questions:*

- Why is the global distribution of wealth and resources considered to be such a problem?
- To what extent have responses to debt cancellation been successful?
- How far do you agree that rich countries have a moral responsibility to help poor countries?
- How strong is the argument that poor countries are responsible for their own problems arising from poverty?
- Why is debt cancellation a moral issue?
- Explain two strengths of religious responses to poverty.
- Explain the benefits that arise out of tackling the problems of poverty.
- To what extent are secular responses to reducing poverty successful?
- Giving examples, assess how successful religious responses have been to tackling the issues created by the unequal distribution of wealth and resources.

| Question Focus | Religious/secular views of NGO work in distribution of wealth and resources |
| --- | --- |

*You need to know:*
- what NGOs are
- religious and secular views of their work
- religious and secular views are often the same
- whether religions can support the work or aims of certain NGOs.

*You need to avoid:*
- sweeping generalisations – let the facts do the talking, not your exaggerations (for the millionth time!)

*You need to look out for:*
- questions that focus on one area of work carried out by NGOs
- questions that ask you to give a view on the success of NGOs.

**Question approaches**

*Statements:*
- 'NGOs can never solve the causes of poverty.'
- 'Everyone has a moral obligation to support the work of NGOs in relation to poverty.'
- 'Religious responses to debt cancellation have been vital in bringing it to public attention.'
- 'NGOs can never solve the problems of poverty until poor countries have political stability.'
- 'The key to overcoming poverty is fairer trade arrangements, not the charitable work of NGOs and religious people.'
- 'Religion does little to help tackle the causes of poverty.'
- 'Religious responses to the global distribution of wealth and resources change nothing.'

*Questions:*
- Why should religious people feel obliged to help the poor?
- How far do you agree that religious people have a moral responsibility to help poor countries?
- How strong is the argument that NGOs can deal only with the effects and not the causes of poverty?
- Why should religious people bother about the poor?
- Explain two strengths of religious responses to poverty.
- Explain the benefits that arise out of tackling the problems of poverty.
- To what extent are secular responses to reducing poverty successful?

| Question Focus | Solutions to problems related to the global distribution of wealth and resources |
|---|---|

*You need to know:*
- what the problems are for the global distribution of wealth and resources

- which solutions have been successful and which have failed.

*You need to avoid:*
- thinking only about the general issue – remember to cover each individual issue
- demanding that your parents distribute their wealth more fairly, especially in your direction.

*You need to look out for:*
- questions that ask you to talk about one solution
- questions that ask you to rate different solutions
- questions that ask you to come up with your own solutions.

**Question approaches**

*Statements:*
- 'The biggest challenge in tackling poverty is removing trading inequality.'
- 'The best solution to the problems of poor countries is political stability'.
- 'The key to overcoming poverty is fairer trade arrangements.'
- 'The blame for poverty lies mainly with rich countries.'
- 'Religion does little to help tackle the causes of poverty.'
- 'Responses to natural disasters do little to change the underlying problems of poverty.'

*Questions:*
- Why are rich countries reluctant to cancel debts of poor countries?
- Why is the global distribution of wealth and resources considered to be such a problem?
- How strong is the argument that poor countries are responsible for their own problems arising from poverty?
- Why is debt cancellation a moral issue?
- Why should religious people feel obliged to argue for debt cancellation?
- Explain two strengths of religious responses to poverty.
- To what extent are secular responses to reducing poverty successful?
- Giving examples, assess how successful religious responses have been to tackling the issues created by the unequal distribution of wealth and resources.

> **Question Focus**    **Strengths and weaknesses of religious/secular responses to the distribution of wealth and resources**

*You need to know:*
- secular and religious responses to the distribution of wealth and resources

- the good and bad points about religious and secular responses
- the effectiveness of both religious and secular responses.

*You need to avoid:*
- focusing on only religious or secular views – you could be asked about both
- sweeping generalisations that are full of accusations against religion.

*You need to look out for:*
- questions that ask you to compare religious and secular responses
- questions that focus on only one area of this topic.

**Question approaches**

*Statements:*
- 'Religious responses to debt cancellation are so few and far between they are not worth bothering about.'
- 'At the very least, religious responses have brought the injustices of the distribution of wealth and resources to everyone's attention.'
- 'Responses to trading inequalities from NGOs and religious groups barely scratch the surface of the issue.'
- 'Religion explains only why there is poverty but it does little about it.'
- 'Religion does little to help tackle the causes of poverty.'

*Questions:*
- How successfully has religion responded to issues arising from the global distribution of wealth and resources?
- Explain why some people consider religious responses to poverty to be weak.
- To what extent have secular responses to debt been successful?
- How far do you agree that religious responses to debt cancellation have been so weak that they are not worth bothering about?
- How can religious and secular groups be more effective in responding to issues arising from the global distribution of wealth and resources?

| Question Focus | Religious and secular views of the benefits and difficulties of different types of aid |
| --- | --- |

*You need to know:*
- what different types of aid are
- at least three or four benefits or difficulties for each
- the benefits and difficulties in some depth, in case the question is about just one of them

- religious and secular views of the benefits and difficulties
- whether the benefits outweigh the difficulties.

*You need to avoid:*
- confusing the different types of aid.

*You need to look out for:*
- questions that ask you for a discussion of one benefit or difficulty
- questions that look for you to rank the benefits or difficulties
- questions that ask you to think about the negative side of the benefits and the positive side of the drawbacks.

**Question approaches**

*Statements:*
- 'Everyone has a moral obligation to support aid.'
- 'Religious people should also give aid, no matter what type.'
- 'Giving money as a form of aid does more harm than good.'
- 'Aid can never solve the problems of poverty.'
- 'Emergency aid fails to tackle the roots of the problems caused by the global distribution of wealth and resources.'
- 'Giving aid simply allows those responsible for poverty to get off the hook.'
- 'In the long term, aid does not really change anything.'

*Questions:*
- Explain two benefits of giving aid.
- Why do some people consider giving aid to be a duty?
- How effective is aid in dealing with the causes of poverty?
- Why should religious people bother about giving aid?
- Why do some people think that giving aid is an easy way of keeping your conscience clear?
- Explain two problems of giving emergency aid.
- Why is long-term aid considered by some people to be more effective than emergency aid?
- How far do you agree that aid should be provided only by secular groups?

# GLOBAL WARMING

| Question Focus | Evaluate religious and secular views or concerns on global warming |
|---|---|

*You need to know:*
- what the problems and issues are for global warming
- who is to blame for the problems arising from global warming
- the moral problems arising from global warming
- religious and secular views of the concerns.

*You need to avoid:*
- focusing only on one aspect of global warming – there's more to it than greenhouse gases
- thinking that a bit of global warming in Scotland might not go amiss.

*You need to look out for:*
- questions that ask you to comment on religious or secular responses
- questions that look for you to assess how accurate religious or secular views are
- questions that ask you whether religious or secular responses are better.

**Question approaches**

*Statements:*
- 'The biggest challenge in tackling global warming is changing public attitudes.'
- 'Without accepting that stewardship of the world is the responsibility of everyone, things will only get worse.'
- 'Human have a duty to care for the world.'
- 'The blame for global warming lies mainly with developed countries.'
- 'Religion does little to help tackle the problems of global warming.'
- 'Global warming is as much about human greed as it is about damaging the environment.'

*Questions:*
- Why is global warming considered to be such a problem?
- To what extent have responses to global warming been successful?
- How far do you agree that developed countries have a moral responsibility to tackle pollution?
- How strong is the argument that poor countries are responsible for global warming?

- Why is pollution a moral issue?
- Why do some religious people feel obliged to argue for a reduction in greenhouse gas emissions?
- Explain two strengths of religious responses to pollution.
- To what extent are secular responses to reducing pollution successful?

| Question Focus | Religious and secular views of NGO work in global warming |
| --- | --- |

*You need to know:*
- what NGOs are
- religious and secular views of their work
- if religions can support the work or aims of certain NGOs.

*You need to avoid:*
- giving the impression that NGOs are useless; they enjoy considerable success.

*You need to look out for:*
- questions that focus on one area of work carried out by NGOs
- questions that ask you to give a view on the success of NGOs.

**Question approaches**

*Statements:*
- 'NGOs can never solve the causes of global warming.'
- 'Everyone has a moral obligation to support the work of NGOs in relation to global warming.'
- 'Global warming is no concern of religion.'
- 'The key to overcoming global warming is recognising that this planet belongs to all life not just human life.'
- 'The concerns of NGOs in relation to global warming are of no concern to religious people.'

*Questions:*
- Why should religious people support the work of NGOs?
- How successful are NGOs in tackling the causes of global warming?
- How far do you agree that religious people have a moral responsibility to support actions against global warming?
- How strong is the argument that NGOs can deal only with effects of global warming and not its causes?

- Explain two strengths of religious responses to actions carried out to tackle global warming.
- Explain the benefits that arise out of tackling pollution.
- To what extent are secular responses to reducing tackling pollution successful?

| Question Focus | Solutions to problems related to global warming |
|---|---|

*You need to know:*
- what the problems are for global warming
- what solutions have been offered
- which solutions have been successful and which have failed.

*You need to avoid:*
- forgetting what 'stewardship' means
- leaving your bedroom window open with the heating on full blast – that's your own personal contribution to global warming!

*You need to look out for:*
- questions that ask you to talk about one solution
- questions that ask you to rate different solutions
- questions that ask you to come up with your own solutions
- questions that ask you to explain why stewardship might be a solution to global warming.

**Question approaches**

*Statements:*
- 'The biggest challenge in tackling global warming is making people care.'
- 'Without strict controls over industrialised countries, pollution will never be removed.'
- 'The abuse of the environment breaks every moral rule in the book.'
- 'The best solution to pollution (hey, a wee rhyme) is to tax the worst polluters the most.'
- 'The cause of pollution is a lack of respect for the environment.'
- 'Religious teachings about the world have contributed to environmental problems; it is unlikely that they can offer any solution to them.'
- 'Whether secular or religious responses; in the long run neither of them will be able to do enough to overcome the problems of global warming.'

*Questions:*

- To what extent can religions be held responsible for the lack of respect towards the environment?
- How far do you agree that industrialised countries have a moral responsibility to tackle pollution?
- How strong is the argument that we need to pollute to maintain our standard of living?
- Why is global warming a moral issue?
- Why should religious people feel obliged to argue for better stewardship of the environment?
- To what extent are secular responses to reducing pollution successful?
- Giving examples, assess how successful religious responses have been in tackling the issues created by global warming.

| Question Focus | Comparisons, benefits and difficulties of religious/ secular responses to global warming |

*You need to know:*

- secular and religious responses to global warming
- the good and bad points about these responses
- the effectiveness of religious and secular responses.

*You need to avoid:*

- forgetting what 'secular' means
- focusing on only religious or secular views – you could be asked about both.

*You need to look out for:*

- questions that ask you to compare religious and secular responses
- questions that focus on only one area of this topic.

**Question approaches**

*Statements:*

- 'Religious responses are less effective than secular responses to issues arising from global warming.'
- 'At the very least, religious responses have made us aware that we have a responsibility to care for the world.'
- 'The most that secular responses can ever achieve is making people aware of the problems caused by pollution.'
- 'Religious and secular groups both agree on how to tackle global warming.'

- 'Religion is concerned only about the afterlife – that is why global warming should not be an issue for it.'

*Questions:*

- How successfully has religion responded to issues arising from global warming?
- Explain why some people consider religious responses to pollution to be weak.
- To what extent have secular responses to global warming been successful?
- Explain the benefits that could arise if religious teaching on stewardship was followed.
- Why might religion be partly to blame for environmental problems?
- How can religious and secular groups be more effective in responding to issues arising from global warming?

# 9   Morality in the modern world – Gender

*Gender issues in the UK*

*Gender issues in the developing world (females)*

## GENDER ISSUES IN THE UK

| Question Focus | Secular (including feminist media views) or religious stereotyping of men and women |
|---|---|

*You need to know:*

- the different ways in which men and women are stereotyped and the problems arising from this
- the different roles of men and women in the home and at work, along with the problems arising from these
- gender issues affecting empowerment and the problems arising from this (Higher only)
- gender issues and the media, and the problems arising from this
- attitudes towards the emancipation of women at home, work and in the media
- criticisms and accuracy of stereotyping.

*You need to avoid:*

- studying only stereotyping of females – it applies to both genders.

*You need to look out for:*

- questions that ask you for a discussion of one particular form of stereotyping – make sure you can write in detail about at least three of the different forms of stereotyping.

**Question approaches**

*Statements:*

- 'Stereotypes of men and women are not so far away from the truth.'

- 'Religion is more guilty of stereotyping men and women than the media.'
- 'Stereotyping should be a cause for concern for everyone.'
- 'Stereotyping causes more good than harm.'

*Questions:*
- Why should stereotyping be a concern for religious people?
- To what extent are women to blame for stereotyping?
- How far do you agree that society needs men and women to adopt their traditional roles?

## Question Focus — Issues created by stereotyping

*You need to know:*
- what issues and problems stereotyping creates
- responses to the issues from religious, secular or feminist groups (if the question is about stereotyping in the media)
- the issues in some depth, in case you get a question that focuses on one particular issue.

*You need to avoid:*
- getting hooked on one issue if the question allows you to discuss more.

*You need to look out for:*
- questions that ask you for a discussion of the issues arising from one particular issue of stereotyping – make sure you can write in detail about at least three of the different forms of stereotyping.

### Question approaches

*Statements:*
- 'Stereotyping is an accurate portrayal of each gender.'
- 'Stereotyping infringes everyone's right to equality.'
- 'Traditional roles of men and women are beneficial to society.'
- 'Stereotyping leads to exploitation.'

*Questions:*
- Why is stereotyping considered to be a problem?
- Why is stereotyping blamed for inequality in society?
- What is the most serious consequence of stereotyping men and women, in your view?

- Is stereotyping such a bad thing?
- Why do some people feel that people over-react to stereotyping?

> **Question Focus**    **Issues raised by the right to have equal opportunities**

*You need to know:*
- the different ways equal opportunities have created issues/had an effect on home life, work and the media in the lives of UK men and women
- the reasons why equal opportunities are considered a right
- the opportunities created by equal opportunities
- each issue in some depth in case you get a question that focuses on just one issue.

*You need to avoid:*
- having a focus on one gender – remember this section can ask about both males and females.

*You need to look out for:*
- questions that ask you for a discussion of one issue related to equal opportunities – make sure you can write in detail about at least three of the different forms of stereotyping
- your dinner flying in your direction, if you happen to tell your mum it is her job to make it.

**Question approaches**

*Statements:*
- 'Because of their different roles in society, opportunities for men and women can never be truly equal.'
- 'Equal opportunities have their drawbacks.'
- 'In the push for equal opportunities, it is men who have lost out.'
- 'Everyone was better off when women stayed at home and men went out to work.'
- 'Men and women have the same rights but different roles.'

*Questions:*
- Why might equality for men and women be a concern for some people?
- Why do many people consider equality to be a good thing?
- To what extent should society be concerned about equal opportunities?
- How far do you agree that men and women are equal but have different roles?
- Has religion got anything to contribute to the gender equality debate?

| Question Focus | Successes and failures and secular and religious views of the Equality and Human Rights Commission (EHRC) |
|---|---|

*You need to know:*
- the ways in which the EHRC has succeeded and failed, and reasons for this
- religious and secular views of the work, and successes and failures of EHRC
- the extent to which religious and secular people can support the EHRC
- the extent to which the EHRC meets its aims.

*You need to avoid:*
- focussing solely on either the successes or the failures of the EHRC – questions could ask about either or both
- portraying religion as being against the EHRC – this is not the case.

*You need to look out for:*
- questions that ask you for a discussion of one issue related to EHRC – make sure you can write in detail about at least three of the different issues related to the EHRC
- questions that are either very negative or very positive about the EHRC – take a middle line on your view, because this is probably the closest to the truth
- questions that ask if religious people can support the EHRC.

**Question approaches**

*Statements:*
- 'The EHRC has been an outstanding success in its promotion of equality for men and women.'
- 'Religious people would have difficulty supporting the aims of the EHRC.'
- 'The EHRC has changed very little in terms of equal opportunities.'
- 'The EHRC undermines the traditional role of men and women in society.'

*Questions:*
- To what extent has the EHRC been successful in achieving its aims?
- How far could a religious person support the aims of the EHRC?
- Explain why it was considered necessary to establish the EHRC.
- Using two examples, explain how the EHRC has improved gender equality in the UK.

> **Question Focus**    **The changing role of men and women at work and in the family**

*You need to know:*
- about traditional roles of men and women at home and at work
- about current and changing roles of men and women at work and in the home and reasons for them
- the improvements and problems these changes have created.

*You need to avoid:*
- being too casual when you prepare for this. Loads of people can talk about it, but talking about it and studying for it are two different things – do not get caught out.

*You need to look out for:*
- questions that ask you to focus on one particular area, i.e. work or home
- questions that ask you why the traditional way is the best way
- a fortnight's washing being dumped on your lap, if you suggest to your mother that traditional roles at home are best.

**Question approaches**

*Statements:*
- 'Women still suffer discrimination at work.'
- 'It is better to have women performing a more traditional role.'
- 'Society has changed for the better as a result of equal opportunities.'
- 'The changing role of men and women in society has not benefited anyone.'
- 'The move to have men take on a more domestic role goes against nature.'

*Questions:*
- Explain two weaknesses of arguments that favour traditional roles for men and women in society.
- To what extent should religion support the traditional role of women in society?
- Using a secular view you have studied, how far do you agree that there are some parts of equal opportunities that do not benefit society as a whole?
- Explain three strengths of men performing their traditional role and going out to work.
- Do you agree that the whole equality issue in the UK has been exaggerated?
- Why is the role of men and women in society such an issue?

**Question Focus** | **Contribution to the religious community**

*You need to know:*
- the roles of and ways in which men and women contribute to all aspects of the religious community (Higher only)
- the ways in which men and women contribute to religious worship (Higher and Int 2)
- the importance of their roles in worship (Int 2 and Higher)
- the reasons for their respective roles in the community (Higher) and in worship (Int 2 and Higher)
- arguments for and against the roles religion gives men and women.

*You need to avoid:*
- (if you are doing Int 2) writing about the general role of women in religious communities – it's not in your course
- writing only about worship at Higher, if the question is a more general question.

*You need to look out for:*
- questions that ask you for a discussion of one issue related to religious worship and community
- questions that look for themes running through religion on its treatment of men and women
- questions that get you to compare religious attitudes with twenty-first-century roles.

**Question approaches**

*Statements:*
- 'Women have a crucial role to play in religious worship.'
- 'Religion is guilty of discriminating against women.'
- 'Only men are suitably qualified to lead religious worship.'
- 'Religion is lagging behind the rest of society in its treatment of women.'
- 'Religious communities have no desire to change with the times in their attitude towards men and women.'

*Questions:*
- Why do some religious people argue that men should play a prominent role in worship?

- Why do some people consider religious attitudes towards men and women outdated?

- Explain why the role of women in religion should be a concern.

- Explain the views of one secular response you have studied to gender equality within one religion.

- Do you agree that religions should have equal roles for men and women in their community?

| Question Focus | Successes and failures of equal opportunities laws, religious and secular views of them |
| --- | --- |

*You need to know:*
- the laws that are easiest and hardest to enforce

- issues arising from the laws

- the successes and failures of the laws

- religious and secular views of the laws

- reasons that religious and secular people can support and criticise the laws.

*You need to avoid:*
- describing the laws without being able to show their strengths, weaknesses, benefits, successes, failures and so on

- stereotyping religious responses to the laws – there is a wide range of responses from religious groups.

*You need to look out for:*
- questions that ask you for a discussion of one issue related to the laws

- questions that look for themes running through the success or failure of the laws

- questions that get you to consider the issues for religion that arise out of the laws.

### Question approaches

*Statements:*
- 'Gender discrimination goes on in spite of the law.'

- 'Discrimination against women is just a natural state of affairs; there's no point having laws against it.'

- 'Discrimination laws have gone too far.'

- 'If it wasn't for Gender Equality laws, women would be in a desperate position.'

*Questions:*
- Why might some religious people argue that discrimination laws are wrong?
- Why do some people consider discrimination laws in the UK to be ineffective?
- Using examples, explain the strengths of UK laws on discrimination.
- Explain the views of one secular response to UK laws on discrimination.

| Question Focus | Religious and secular concerns about gender issues in the UK |
|---|---|

*You need to know:*
- issues related to stereotyping in the media, empowerment, gender roles and equal opportunities
- reasons why religious and secular people are concerned about the various issues
- how religious and secular groups might contribute to and tackle the issues
- differences between religious and secular approaches
- that religious and secular approaches to the issues can have much in common.

*You need to avoid:*
- focusing on just one issue; you need them all and you need to know what is said and done about them by religious and secular groups.

*You need to look out for:*
- questions that ask you for a discussion of one issue
- questions that look for themes running through the issues
- questions that get you to consider whether religion should respond positively or negatively to the issues.

**Question approaches**

*Statements:*
- 'Media stereotyping is as bad for men as it is for women.'
- 'It is better to have women performing a more traditional role.'
- 'The changing role of men and women in society has not benefited anyone.'
- 'The push for equality has been done at the expense of the family.'

*Questions:*
- Why do some religious people argue that women should focus on their traditional role in the home?
- Explain two weaknesses of arguments that favour traditional roles for men and women in society.

- To what extent should religion support the traditional role of women in society?
- Explain three strengths of men performing their traditional role and going out to work.
- Give two reasons why some people feel that religion should promote gender equality.
- How successful are arguments against media stereotyping?

| Question Focus | Religious and secular views of the benefits and difficulties of equal opportunities |
|---|---|

*You need to know:*
- what 'equal opportunities' means
- the benefits and difficulties in some depth in case they ask you about just one of them
- religious and secular views of the benefits and difficulties
- religious and secular views are often the same
- whether the benefits outweigh the difficulties.

*You need to avoid:*
- focusing only on the laws relating to equal opportunities – remember that equal opportunities affect society in many ways aside from the law
- sweeping generalisations that are full of accusations against religion.

*You need to look out for:*
- questions that ask you for a discussion of one benefit or difficulty
- questions that look for you to rank the benefits or difficulties
- questions that ask you to think about the negative side of the benefits and the positive side of the drawbacks.

**Question approaches**

*Statements:*
- 'The benefits of gender equality far outweigh the difficulties caused by them.'
- 'Society benefits greatly from the traditional role of women in the home.'
- 'The major drawback of gender equality is that it fails to take the differences between men and women into account.'
- 'The changing role of men and women in society has not benefited anyone.'
- 'Gender equality has created difficulties for families.'

*Questions:*
- Explain two advantages of gender equality for men.
- Explain two weaknesses of arguments that support gender equality.
- Using examples, explain two obstacles to achieving gender equality in the UK.
- Why are equal opportunities considered essential in the UK today?
- Give two reasons why some people feel that equal opportunities have gone too far.

# GENDER ISSUES IN THE DEVELOPING WORLD (FEMALES)

| Question Focus | Religious and secular view on the effectiveness and impact of UN Declarations and the Beijing Platform for Action |
|---|---|

*You need to know:*
- what each UN action is
- problems and issues faced by the UN in implementation
- reasons for effectiveness and ineffectiveness
- religious and secular views of the effectiveness and impact
- whether religion has, in any way, contributed to the success or failure of the UN's work.

*You need to avoid:*
- focusing on only one response of the UN – you could be asked to write about them all
- sweeping generalisations that are damning of the UN's work, which has, in fact, experienced some success.

*You need to look out for:*
- questions that ask you for a discussion of one benefit or difficulty or aspect of effectiveness
- questions that look for you to rank the benefits or difficulties
- questions that ask you to think about the negative side of the benefits and the positive side of the drawbacks.

**Question approaches**

*Statements:*
- 'The UN response to gender issues in the developing world is too little too late.'

- 'The work of the UN in supporting women in the developing world really has made a difference.'
- 'The Beijing Platform for Action has achieved very little.'
- 'Different cultures should be left to sort out their own gender issues.'
- 'UN support for women in the developing world is not universally accepted.'
- 'Religious people should support the aims of the Beijing Platform for Action.'
- 'Religious people should feel morally obliged to support the work of the UN on women in the developing world.'

*Questions:*

- How effective do you consider UN responses to gender issues in the developing world to be?
- Why do some people consider the UN to be ineffective in tackling the problems of women in the developing world?
- How far do you agree with the view that the UN will always have to fight to protect women in the developing world?
- Why does the UN consider it necessary to support women in the developing world?
- How successfully has the UN dealt with concerns relating to women in the developing world?
- To what extent should the UN's support of women in the developing world be a concern for religious people?
- How far do you agree that the UN responses to issues concerning women in the developing world should be supported by both religious and secular groups?

| Question Focus | Religious and secular views, responses or concerns about the problems facing women in the developing world |
| --- | --- |

*You need to know:*

- what the problems are
- the problems in detail, in case you are asked to comment on just one
- the causes and effects of the problem
- the views of religious and secular groups
- how religious and secular groups contribute to or tackle the problem
- religious and secular views of what should be done
- religious and secular actions.

*You need to avoid:*
- focusing on only one problem – you could be asked to talk about them all
- sweeping generalisations that blame religion for all the world's problems.

*You need to look out for:*
- questions that ask you for a discussion of one benefit or difficulty, or religious or secular response
- going over the top in discussing violence against women – without wanting to detract from a serious issue, there is a danger that you could lean too much on this
- questions that look for you to discuss the good and bad points of religious or secular views or responses – these can be phrased in loads of different ways.

**Question approaches**

*Statements:*
- 'The biggest challenge facing women in the developing world today is their education.'
- 'Without proper education and health care, women in the developing world will never make progress.'
- 'Trafficking in women breaks every moral rule in the book.'
- 'The best solution to the problems facing women in the developing world is to improve their education.'
- 'Keeping things the same for women in the developing world is not an option.'
- 'Religion makes matters worse for women in the developing world, not better.'
- 'Religious responses to the situation of women in the developing world make a positive difference.'

*Questions:*
- In your view, explain what the biggest challenge facing women in the developing world is.
- Why is the health of women in the developing world such an important issue?
- To what extent have responses to the trafficking of women been successful?
- How strong is the evidence that things are improving for women in the developing world?
- Why is the empowerment of women in the developing world a moral problem?

- Why are the issues facing women in the developing world considered to be a moral issue?
- Explain two strengths of religious responses to health issues facing women in the developing world.
- Explain the benefits for women that arise out of responses to female empowerment.
- To what extent is the secular response to trafficking successful?
- Giving examples, assess how successful religious responses have been in tackling the issues faced by women in the developing world.

# 10 Morality in the modern world – Medical ethics

*Use of embryos*

*Euthanasia*

## USE OF EMBRYOS

| Question Focus | Religious and secular views on the status of the embryo and their strengths and weaknesses |
|---|---|

*You need to know:*
- secular and religious views on when life begins
- the good/bad points about their responses
- criticisms and support of their positions.

*You need to avoid:*
- confusing religious with secular views.

*You need to look out for:*
- questions that ask you to compare religious and secular responses
- questions that focus on only one definition of the beginning of life
- questions that ask why the status of the embryo is such a big deal.

**Question approaches**

*Statements:*
- 'Religious views on the status of the embryo are unhelpful.'
- 'It's time we got over this love affair with the human embryo. It is not human. End of story.'
- 'The embryo deserves the benefit of the doubt.'
- 'God has willed every embryo to exist therefore nothing may be done to harm them.'

- 'Whatever way you look at it, the embryo is a living thing and it is being harmed.'
- 'The embryo is a potential human. Nothing more and nothing less.'
- 'The benefits that arise from using embryos are so great that concerns about their status should be put to one side.'

*Questions:*
- Why might some religious people consider the embryo to be human?
- Why is the status of the embryo a moral issue?
- The key issue in the debate about the status of embryos is about how they can benefit humanity. Do you agree?
- Why is the status of the embryo considered to be an important issue?
- Explain why some religious people can accept limited embryo use.
- Why do some people consider the embryo not to be human?

---

**Question Focus** | **Issues related to playing God, and the slippery slope**

---

*You need to know:*
- the slippery slope argument
- the playing God argument
- why some people see the slippery slope and playing God being a problem in this issue
- criticisms and support of both these arguments
- that religious and secular views can have the same view of these arguments.

*You need to avoid:*
- forgetting about the slippery slope – you could break your arm!
- confusing the slippery slope argument with the playing God argument.

*You need to look out for:*
- questions that ask you about the risks attached to embryo usage
- questions that ask you to defend the slippery slope or playing God arguments
- questions that ask why either of these should be a concern
- questions asking why playing God might be a concern for secular organisations.

**Question approaches**

*Statements:*
- 'Using embryos for any purpose is inviting trouble.'

- 'The problem with using embryos is that science will always want to push the boundaries.'
- 'If embryo use is declared wrong then we have no need to worry about where it will go next.'
- 'We do not have the right to play God with embryos.'
- 'Using embryos is taking human power too far.'
- 'If embryo use is playing God, wouldn't God want to use embryos to save lives?'
- 'Slippery slopes are dangerous. You have no idea where you will end up. That is why embryo use for any purpose is wrong.'

*Questions:*

- Why might some religious people object to using embryos?
- How strong is the playing God argument?
- To what extent is the slippery slope argument against the use of embryos successful?
- Explain two strengths of the slippery slope argument in relation to the use of embryos.
- Why is the playing God argument on embryo usage considered to be a weak argument?
- Why might some secular views include the playing God argument in their view on embryo use?

| **Question Focus** | **Religious and secular views on IVF and their strengths and weaknesses** |
|---|---|

*You need to know:*

- secular and religious views on IVF
- the good and bad points about their responses
- criticisms and support of their positions.

*You need to avoid:*

- lumping all religious views on IVF together – there is disagreement you know!

*You need to look out for:*

- questions that ask you to discuss specific uses of IVF
- questions that ask you to compare religious and secular views on one use of IVF
- questions that ask why the status of the embryo is important in the debate about IVF.

## Question approaches

*Statements:*

- 'IVF takes interference a step too far.'
- 'No religious person could accept IVF because it is against God's will.'
- 'If everyone has the chance to benefit from IVF in some way, then it is morally right.'
- 'Anything that interferes with the natural process of reproduction can never be right.'
- 'If we can benefit from IVF then we ought to use it.'
- 'Religious views on IVF do nothing other than hold back progress in medical science.'

*Questions:*

- To what extent do you agree that everyone has the right to have children, whether by natural means or through IVF?
- Why do some religious people object to IVF?
- Why are some secular views on IVF opposed to some religious views on IVF?
- How far do you agree that IVF has to be controlled by law?
- Explain the common concerns of some religious and secular views on IVF.
- Is it fair to say that religious arguments against IVF are weak?
- Assess the strengths of two secular views on IVF.

| Question Focus | Religious and secular views on stem cell research and their strengths and weaknesses |
| --- | --- |

*You need to know:*

- secular and religious views on stem cell research
- what adult and embryo stem cell research are
- the successes and failures of stem cell research
- the good and bad points about religious and secular arguments
- criticisms and support of religious and secular positions.

*You need to avoid:*

- getting too wrapped up in arguments about whether the embryo is human or not.

*You need to look out for:*

- questions that ask you to weigh up the benefits and drawbacks of stem cell research from a religious or secular perspective

- questions that focus on religious and secular views of the alternatives to stem cell research
- questions that ask why the status of the embryo is such a big deal in relation to stem cell research.

**Question approaches**

*Statements:*
- 'No religious person could accept stem cell research.'
- 'Stem cell research is using a person as a means to an end.'
- 'If everyone has the chance to benefit from stem cell research in some way, then it is morally right.'
- 'If we can benefit from stem cell research then we ought to use it.'
- 'Religious views on stem cell research do nothing other than hold back progress in medical science.'

*Questions:*
- To what extent do you agree that, if stem cell research is available, we should use it?
- Why do some religious people object to stem cell research?
- Why do some people feel that stem cell research is unnecessary?
- Is it fair to say that religious arguments against stem cell research are strong?
- Assess the weaknesses of two secular views on stem cell research.

| **Question Focus** | **Religious and secular views on genetic selection/PGD or PGS and their strengths and weaknesses** |
| --- | --- |

*You need to know:*
- the uses of genetic selection or screening
- secular and religious views on genetic selection or screening
- the meaning of eugenics
- religious and secular views of eugenics
- the good and bad points about these views
- criticisms and support of religious and secular views.

*You need to avoid:*
- having too much of a focus on the Nazi-type implications of embryo selection – it's very easy to end up writing tons on this when you don't have to.

*You need to look out for:*
- questions that ask you to compare religious and secular responses

- questions that focus on only one use of genetic selection or screening
- questions that ask why genetic screening or selection is such a big issue.

**Question approaches**

*Statements:*
- 'PGD is worth it if it prevents suffering.'
- 'No religious person could accept PGD because it is against God's will.'
- 'If everyone has the chance to benefit from PGD in some way, then it is morally right.'
- 'PGD should be the duty of all people who are starting a family.'
- 'PGD is just a form of creating designer babies and is wrong for that reason.'

*Questions:*
- To what extent do you agree that everyone has the right to have the child they want even if it means using PGD?
- Why do some religious people object to PGD?
- Explain the common concerns of some religious and secular views on PGD.
- To what extent do you agree that decisions arising from PGD are nobody's business apart from the parents'?
- Are the fears about eugenics and PGD justified?

| Question Focus | Religious and secular views on saviour siblings and their strengths and weaknesses |
| --- | --- |

*You need to know:*
- the uses of saviour siblings
- secular and religious views on saviour siblings
- the good and bad points about these positions
- criticisms and support of both of these positions.

*You need to avoid:*
- writing loads about *My Sister's Keeper*, because (a) it is just a story, (b) you will smudge the ink on your paper if you try to describe the movie because it's a bit of a weepie! (Apologies to those who have not seen it.)

*You need to look out for:*
- questions that ask you to compare religious and secular responses
- questions that focus only on the benefits of saviour siblings
- questions that ask whether this kind of technology is using a person solely as a means to an end.

## Question approaches

*Statements:*

- 'A child should be conceived for the love of it, not because it can be a spare part for an existing child.'

- 'There is no worse abuse of an embryo than creating one for the purposes of another child's treatment.'

- 'No person should feel as though he or she has been conceived because he or she is useful for spare parts.'

- 'The worst thing about saviour siblings is that the embryo has no choice in the matter.'

- 'Creating saviour siblings removes God's right to will every life into existence.'

- 'What better a reason can there be to be born than to save another person?'

*Questions:*

- To what extent do you agree that creating saviour siblings ignores the rights of the individual?

- Why do some religious people object to saviour siblings?

- Why do some secular views support saviour siblings?

- Explain the common concerns of some religious and secular views on saviour siblings.

- Why might the rights of the individual be threatened through the creation of saviour siblings?

- Explain what concern about saviour siblings will bother religious people the most.

| Question Focus | Religious and secular views concerns on the issues surrounding UK laws on embryo use |
|---|---|

*You need to know:*

- the HFE Act 2008 (and any changes made to it after 2008)

- the work of the HFEA

- what changes have been made to the act and why

- criticisms of and support for the HFE Act 2008 and the HFEA

- secular and religious views on the Act and HFEA

- the good and bad points about religious and secular responses

- criticisms and support of religious and secular positions.

*You need to avoid:*
- saying that religions are dead against the HFE Act and the HFEA – many say that they are better than nothing at all.

*You need to look out for:*
- questions that ask whether or not religious people can support the Act or HFEA
- questions that focus on only one aspect of the Act or HFEA
- questions that ask why the HFEA is necessary – and don't exaggerate the reasons for this.

**Question approaches**

*Statements:*
- 'The HFE Act has opened the door to abuses of embryos.'
- 'The work of the HFEA successfully controls potential abuses of the HFE Act.'
- 'Religious people should be grateful that, at the very least, we have the HFE Act to control embryo use.'
- 'The HFE Act is guilty of assuming that an embryo is not human. Therefore it is immoral.'
- 'Changes to the HFE Act just go to show that we are on the slippery slope as far as the use of embryos goes.'

*Questions:*
- To what extent do you agree that the HFE Act is morally acceptable?
- Why do some religious people object to the existence of laws on human embryos?
- Why might some scientists object to the HFE Act and the work of the HFEA?
- How far do you agree that embryo use has to be controlled by law?
- Explain why some religious people feel that current UK laws on embryo use are the lesser of two evils.
- Is it fair to say that religious arguments against embryo laws are weak?
- Assess the strength of two secular views on the work of the HFEA.

# EUTHANASIA

| Question Focus | Religious and secular views on, or concerns about, euthanasia |
|---|---|

*You need to know:*
- the different types and methods of euthanasia, including double effect

- secular and religious views on the different types and methods of euthanasia
- the good and bad points about their responses
- criticisms and support of their positions.

*You need to avoid:*
- saying that religions support euthanasia because they accept double effect – that is not how religions see it as a whole
- thinking that euthanasia is a country.

*You need to look out for:*
- questions that ask you to compare religious and secular responses
- questions that focus on only one type or method of euthanasia
- questions that ask why religious people might support euthanasia.

**Question approaches**

*Statements:*
- 'To deny a person voluntary euthanasia is to deny a person their human right to make decisions about their own future.'
- 'Non voluntary euthanasia is killing the defenceless.'
- 'Double effect is nothing but a convenient name for euthanasia by the back door.'
- 'A right that is more important than the right to life is the right not to be killed – euthanasia denies people that right.'
- 'How can anyone in this day and age justify continuing the suffering of someone who does not want to live?'
- 'God gives life and only God can take it away.'
- 'The fact that religion accepts "double effect" goes to show that, in fact, they approve of euthanasia.'
- 'Passive voluntary or non voluntary euthanasia should be the only way that euthanasia is carried out.'

*Questions:*
- Why might religious people consider 'double effect' to be morally acceptable but euthanasia to be wrong?
- Should the BMA have any position at all on euthanasia?
- Why is non-voluntary euthanasia considered to be more of a problem by some people than voluntary euthanasia?
- In general, religions are against euthanasia. However, why might some religious people be sympathetic towards arguments in its favour?

- Why do some religious people object to arguments supporting euthanasia?
- Explain two weaknesses of religious arguments against voluntary euthanasia.
- Why do some people consider secular arguments in favour of euthanasia to be very persuasive?

| Question Focus | Secular and religious views and concerns about issues relating to UK/Netherlands laws |
|---|---|

*You need to know:*
- the UK and Netherlands laws
- the moral issues arising from euthanasia
- religious and secular views of the laws
- the good and bad points about their responses
- criticisms and support of their positions.

*You need to avoid:*
- lumping all the UK laws together because there are some differences
- confusing voluntary and non-voluntary euthanasia.

*You need to look out for:*
- questions that ask you to compare religious and secular responses
- questions that focus on only one set of laws
- questions that ask which set of laws is more acceptable for religion
- questions that ask why euthanasia laws are such a big deal.

**Question approaches**

*Statements:*
- 'The UK deals with situations relating to euthanasia in the best way possible.'
- 'Euthanasia laws in the Netherlands are simply a licence to kill.'
- 'By law, everyone has the right to life so, by law, everyone should have the right to die when they want to.'
- 'The laws in the Netherlands do not protect the vulnerable.'
- 'The UK's reluctance to have laws permitting euthanasia is helpful to no-one.'
- 'No religious person should accept the Netherlands' laws on euthanasia.'

*Questions:*
- Why are euthanasia laws so controversial?
- How far do you agree that Scotland should seriously consider legalising physician-assisted suicide?

- Is it fair to say that, if the UK made euthanasia legal, every vulnerable person would then be at risk?
- Explain why some people feel that religious arguments against legalising euthanasia are fair and justified.
- What are the merits of the arguments in favour of legalising euthanasia?
- How might religious people reply to criticisms of their position on legalising euthanasia?

| Question Focus | Religious and secular views on and responses to palliative care |
| --- | --- |

*You need to know:*
- what palliative care is
- secular and religious views on palliative care
- arguments for and against palliative care
- the benefits and difficulties of palliative care
- religious and secular views on the need for euthanasia when there is palliative care
- the good/bad points about their responses
- criticisms and support of their positions.

*You need to avoid:*
- sweeping generalisations – there is a wide range of views within different religions although they do tend to support high-quality palliative care.

*You need to look out for:*
- questions that ask you for moral issues arising from palliative care
- questions that ask you why it is the preferred choice of some people
- questions that ask why palliative care is supported by religious people and medical organisations
- questions that ask you if palliative care is worth the effort.

**Question approaches**

*Statements:*
- 'Palliative care is the best way possible to care for the dying.'
- 'The experience in the Netherlands is that most people opt for palliative care – this shows euthanasia is unnecessary.'
- 'Palliative care is expensive and a drain on scarce resources; euthanasia should be the main option for the dying.'

- 'Palliative care benefits only individuals who are suffering.'
- 'Palliative care hits all the right notes with religious views on caring for the dying.'

*Questions:*
- Why is palliative care considered by some to be controversial?
- How far do you agree that palliative care is too much of a drain on resources with little in the way of a return?
- Why have the hospice movement's ideals become attractive to many people?
- What are the merits in the argument for high quality palliative care to be available for all?
- How might religious people argue that palliative care is the only morally acceptable way to support the dying?

# 11 Morality in the modern world – War and peace

Responses to war

Modern armaments

## RESPONSES TO WAR

| Question Focus | Religious and secular views of pacifism, criticism and support for pacifism |
|---|---|

*You need to know:*
- the main points for and against different types of pacifism
- strengths and weaknesses of different types of pacifism.

*You need to avoid:*
- confusing different types of pacifism.

*You need to look out for:*
- questions that ask for a religious or secular response to pacifism.

**Question approaches**

*Statements:*
- 'Pacifism is simply another word for 'cowardice'.'
- 'Nothing will end war unless the people themselves refuse to go to war.'

*Albert Einstein*

- 'Absolute pacifism is simply an invitation to lawlessness the world over.'
- 'Absolute pacifism is as morally wrong as declaring war.'
- 'Pacifism is wonderful in theory, but totally impractical in today's world.'
- 'War is necessary. Pacifism is unnecessary.'
- 'Pacifism is a sign of strength, not weakness.'

*Questions:*
- Why is pacifism criticised by some people?
- Why might some religious people support pacifism?
- To what extent is pacifism successful as a response to war?
- How far do you agree that a conditional pacifist is not really a pacifist at all?
- Do you agree that the only true pacifist is an absolute pacifist?
- Explain one strength of pacifism in depth.
- How far do you agree that the criticisms of pacifism outweigh its merits?

## Question Focus — Benefits/drawbacks of war

*You need to know:*
- the benefits and drawbacks of war.

*You need to avoid:*
- thinking that benefits and drawbacks belong to two separate categories – what some people call a benefit might be drawback for other people and vice versa.

*You need to look out for:*
- questions that ask if the benefits or drawbacks outweigh each other because you might feel you have to come down on one side or the other – take the middle line as there's a lot to say there
- questions that focus on one particular drawback or benefit.

**Question approaches**

*Statements:*
- 'Wars are a necessary evil.'
- 'No war can ever be justified.'
- 'Wars in themselves are not wrong but the way they are fought might be.'
- 'War will exist until that distant day when the conscientious objector enjoys the same reputation and prestige that the warrior does today.'

*John F. Kennedy*

- 'There is no such thing as a good war and a bad peace.'

*Questions:*
- Explain two major benefits that arise from war.
- Why do some people see war as something that is necessary?
- To what extent is war something that can only be bad?

- How far do you agree that nothing is really gained from war?
- Why might some religious people consider war to be right?
- Would it be fair to say that the drawbacks of war are greater than the benefits of war?

| Question Focus | Evaluation of reasons for going to war from religious and secular perspectives |
|---|---|

*You need to know:*
- what the religious and secular views are
- why religious and secular groups are concerned about going to war
- the strengths and weaknesses of both religious and secular arguments.

*You need to avoid:*
- writing generally about the good and bad reasons for going to war, if the question asks specifically for religious or secular views of the reasons
- arguing that stealing a cadbury's caramel from your selection box is a good reason for declaring war on your sibling.

*You need to look out for:*
- questions that ask for a religious view – your answer will contain loads of secular insights that are shared with religious people but, if you can, find a couple of things that are clearly religious
- questions that focus on one particular reason for going to war and whether it could be justified by a religious person
- questions about religious and secular reasons for not going to war.

**Question approaches**

*Statements:*
- 'Wars should only be fought in self-defence.'
- 'Every nation has a duty to protect other nations from rulers who abuse their human rights.'
- 'Pre-emptive strikes are the best form of defence.'
- 'Wars today are all about rich nations protecting their investments in small nations.'
- 'God does not want war, so religious people should never get involved.'
- 'There are no acceptable reasons for going to war.'

*Questions:*
- Why might some religious people consider that war can never be justified?

- Explain a secular view that supports the fighting of wars.
- To what extent do you agree that changing the government of another country can never be an acceptable reason for going to war?
- How far does the evil of war prevent even greater evils taking place?
- Should religious people fight in wars?

| Question Focus | Religious and secular views, criticism and support for international Conventions |
|---|---|

*You need to know:*
- what the Conventions are
- at least three criticisms and supporting views of each Convention you have studied
- what themes run through the Conventions
- the effectiveness of the Conventions
- religious and secular views
- the strengths and weaknesses of both religious and secular views.

*You need to avoid:*
- confusing the Conventions.

*You need to look out for:*
- questions that focus on the themes running through the Conventions, because they are looking for an overview
- questions that might focus on one Convention and its strengths and weaknesses
- questions that ask for a religious view – your answer will contain loads of secular insights that are shared with religious people but you need to find a couple of things that are clearly religious
- questions that focus on one particular aspect of the Conventions from a religious or secular perspective
- questions that ask if religious people could support the Conventions.

**Question approaches**

*Statements:*
- 'If it wasn't for international Conventions on war, nobody would be safe.'
- 'The only Conventions worth bothering about are those that protect civilians.'
- 'International Conventions on war are a failure because they basically say that it is acceptable to go to war.'

- 'International Conventions on war have been shown time and again to be ineffective.'
- 'International Conventions on war create as many moral problems as they solve.'

*Questions:*
- Explain why some religious people might have concerns about international Conventions on war.
- How successfully are international Conventions on war enforced?
- To what extent are international Conventions on war necessary?
- Why should prisoners of war have their rights respected?
- Is it fair to say that the fact that international Conventions exist shows that the world agrees that war is morally acceptable?

# MODERN ARMAMENTS

| Question Focus | Role of WMDs in war (no chemical or biological weapons at Int 2) |
|---|---|

*You need to know:*
- what WMD are and their uses, e.g. deterrents
- how effective or ineffective they are in war or when war threatens.

*You need to avoid:*
- saying that children are the most effective WMDs known to humanity.

*You need to look out for:*
- questions that ask how WMDs can promote peace
- questions that ask how successfully they have been used in negotiations for peace
- questions that ask if it is moral to have them as part of any peace process or war.

**Question approaches**

*Statements:*
- 'A world without nuclear weapons would be less stable and more dangerous for all of us.'

*Margaret Thatcher*
- 'If you possess WMDs then you must intend using them if necessary.'

- 'Nuclear weapons are a necessary evil.'
- 'There have been no world wars since 1945 because of nuclear weapons.'
- 'Nations have a duty to defend their people with the most effective weapons at their disposal.'
- 'The threat of nuclear attack keeps rogue leaders under control.'

*Questions:*
- Explain the role of nuclear weapons in maintaining peace.
- Why do some people say that nuclear weapons are necessary?
- Explain two drawbacks of possessing nuclear weapons.
- To what extent is it possible for a religious person to support the possession and use of WMDs?
- World War II ended shortly after the USA dropped nuclear bombs on Japan. Explain the moral issues created by this decision.
- Is it morally acceptable for WMDs to play any role in wars?

| Question Focus | Religious or secular justification for possessing and using conventional and non-conventional weapons |
| --- | --- |

*You need to know:*
- what the religious and secular views are – you will find that they may be similar, and it is a good thing to point this out.
- why religious and secular groups are concerned about possessing and using WMDs
- religious and secular views on the use and possession of conventional weapons
- religious and secular views on the benefits and drawbacks of possessing and using WMDs
- religious and secular views on the benefits and drawbacks of possessing and using conventional weapons.

*You need to avoid:*
- generalising religious views on WMDs in particular
- confusing conventional and non-conventional weapons
- confusing possession with use.

*You need to look out for:*
- questions that ask if peace would be possible without the deterrent of WMDs
- questions that focus on the use or possession of one particular type of weapon, from a religious or secular perspective

- questions that ask if religious people could support international conventions and agreements.

## Question approaches

*Statements:*
- 'A war fought with WMDs can never be moral.'
- 'If wars have to be fought then it should be only with conventional weapons.'
- 'Possession of WMDs is just as bad as using them.'
- 'Possession of any weapons is morally wrong because both WMDs and conventional weapons demonstrate the intention to kill.'
- 'Leaders of nations would be failing in their duty to defend their people if they did not possess WMDs.'
- 'Religious people could never ever support the possession of nuclear weapons.'
- 'Conventional weapons are the only weapons that any nation should ever have.'

*Questions:*
- Compare religious and secular views on the use of WMDs.
- To what extent is the use of WMDs morally acceptable in some cases?
- Can the deployment of WMDs ever be morally justifiable?
- Why are conventional weapons considered to be more acceptable than WMDs?
- Give an explanation of two strengths in arguments that support the use of conventional weapons only.
- Why might the use of conventional weapons create moral problems for some religious people?

# 12 World religions – Buddhism

*The human condition*

*The goals of life*

*The means to the goals*

## THE HUMAN CONDITION

**Question Focus** | Buddhist view of the human condition: pessimistic or realistic

*You need to know:*
- the various aspects of the human condition
- the general characteristics of the human condition, e.g. suffering, death, impermanence, desire
- which aspects of the human condition are negative, positive and realistic
- how Buddhists' views compare with actual experience.

*You need to avoid:*
- taking one side – try to be balanced when the question permits.

*You need to look out for:*
- any words in questions on this theme, which could mean positive, negative, realistic, unrealistic – you use the same information
- the term 'human condition' – you must know what it means
- questions that focus on one aspect of the human condition.

**Question approaches**

*Statements:*
- 'Buddhist views of the human condition are very pessimistic.'
- 'Buddhist views of the human condition give an accurate description of it.'

- 'Life is not as bad as Buddhist understandings make it out to be.'
- 'There is little evidence that the Buddhist view of the human condition is either fair or accurate.'
- 'Buddhist views of life devalue its meaning and importance.'
- 'Buddhists say that all life is suffering; nothing can be further from the truth.'
- 'Belief in anatta renders human life totally pointless.'

*Questions:*
- To what extent are Buddhists' views of the human condition negative?
- Why might some people view Buddhist teaching on anicca as a negative teaching?
- How important is belief in anatta in understanding the human condition?
- Why is samsara considered to be an important aspect of Buddhist beliefs about the human condition?
- Why is the Buddhist view of the human condition considered to be realistic?

| **Question Focus** | **Positive and negative effects of the human condition on Buddhists** |
| --- | --- |

*You need to know:*
- the various aspects of the human condition
- the general characteristics of the human condition, e.g. suffering, death, impermanence and desire
- which aspects of the human condition have a good/bad effect on people
- what problems the different aspects of the human condition can create for people.

*You need to avoid:*
- seeing the Buddhist view of human life as being entirely negative.

*You need to look out for:*
- questions that refer to how Buddhists feel about the human condition
- the term 'human condition' – you must know what it means
- questions that focus on one aspect of the human condition.

**Question approaches**

*Statements:*
- 'Buddhist teachings on the nature of human beings offer hope.'
- 'Belief in anatta is enough to make a person want to give up.'

- 'There is nothing attractive in the belief that we have no soul.'
- 'There are no positives that can be taken out of the belief that all life is suffering.'
- 'We are nothing more than the Five Skandhas.'
- 'Samsara offers hope to all Buddhists.'
- 'Controlling the Three Poisons bring benefits both to individuals and the community.'

*Questions:*

- Why is belief in samsara a positive belief for many Buddhists?
- How important is control of the Three Poisons in the quest for nibbana?
- Why might Buddhists disagree that their view of the human condition is negative?
- To what extent does Buddhist belief in impermanence affect their lives?
- Do you agree that the greatest challenge of the human condition is tanha?

| Question Focus | **Centrality of individual concepts to the human condition (including the relationship between different concepts and different aspects being the key to understanding it)** |
|---|---|

*You need to know:*

- the various aspects of the human condition
- the general characteristics of the human condition, e.g. suffering, death, impermanence desire
- how the different aspects of the human condition are related to each other
- how they can all be central in some way.

*You need to avoid:*

- missing out one of the aspects in your discussion of centrality
- disagreeing with centrality questions if you can avoid it – the best thing is to argue is that none is more central than the other, and go on to show how they are interrelated
- giving a description of the human condition without mentioning centrality – it will get you no marks.
- your teacher, if you do a religion other than the one you have studied!

*You need to look out for:*

- the different ways in which centrality-type questions can be asked
- the term 'human condition' – you must know what it means

- questions that focus on one aspect of the human condition and ask about its centrality
- questions that ask you to discuss two or more related aspects of the human condition.

**Question approaches**

*Statements:*
- 'Tanha is central to Buddhist understandings of the human condition.'
- 'Anatta is at the heart of Buddhist teachings on the human condition.'
- 'Understanding anicca is more important than understanding any other part of the human condition.'
- 'If Buddhists do not accept that all life is dukkha, then they have no chance of understanding the human condition.'
- 'The Three Root Poisons are the cause of dukkha.'
- 'The beauty of Buddhist understandings of the human condition is the way all the concepts are connected to each other.'
- 'Anatta makes samsara impossible to work.'
- 'Anicca is the sole cause of dukkha.'

*Questions:*
- To what extent are the Five Skandhas central to the human condition?
- For Buddhists, what is the key aspect of the human condition?
- How far do you agree that the Three Marks of Existence are at the centre of Buddhist understandings of the human condition?
- How successfully can it be argued that impermanence is at the heart of Buddhist understandings of the human condition?
- Why is the Second Noble Truth such an important aspect of the human condition?
- To what extent are the Three Root Poisons the cause of dukkha?

| Question Focus | Benefits and difficulties of overcoming the human condition |
|---|---|

*You need to know:*
- the various aspects of the human condition
- the benefits and difficulties of each one
- the ways in which each one can be overcome (means to the goals)
- how to overcome the problems caused by the human condition

- why it might be difficult/easy to overcome these difficulties
- in what ways the benefits might help individuals or society.

*You need to avoid:*
- writing about the centrality of different aspects of the human condition – this question is not about that
- getting different aspects of the human condition mixed up.

*You need to look out for:*
- questions that focus on one or two aspects of the human condition and ask you to discuss them in relation to benefits and difficulties
- questions that look for some kind of comparison of the benefits and difficulties
- questions that state a benefit or difficulty and you have to explain it.

**Question approaches**

*Statements:*
- 'Once Buddhists understand the human condition, their suffering ends.'
- 'The main benefits of overcoming the human condition are seen more in the individual rather than the community.'
- 'The problem with overcoming the human condition is that you have to go against everything your senses tell you.'
- 'There seems to be little point to life for Buddhists once they have understood the human condition.'
- 'Destroying the effects of the Three Root Poisons is the main benefit from understanding the human condition.'

*Questions:*
- Explain the main benefits for Buddhists of overcoming the human condition.
- Why might it be argued that there is nothing attractive about overcoming the human condition?
- Explain the difficulties Buddhists might have in overcoming the Three Root Poisons.
- Why might understanding the Three Marks of Existence bring benefits to Buddhists?

| Question Focus | Benefits, drawbacks, difficulties, effect and role of samsara |
| --- | --- |

*You need to know:*
- how samsara works

- the benefits, drawbacks and effects of samsara
- where it fits into the human condition/Buddhism as a whole.

*You need to avoid:*
- simply giving a description of how samsara works – if it's an AE question, keep it that way!

*You need to look out for:*
- questions that focus on one or two aspects of samsara and ask you to discuss them
- questions that are very negative about samsara.

**Question approaches**

*Statements:*
- 'Samsara puts everyone in charge of their own destiny.'
- 'Samsara can benefit both the individual and the community.'
- 'The belief in samsara does not work because Buddhists teach about anatta.'
- 'Belief in samsara is worthwhile only if the individual survives death.'
- 'Samsara makes no difference to the lives of ordinary Buddhists.'

*Questions:*
- How can samsara make sense if Buddhists believe in anatta?
- Explain the two benefits of believing in samsara.
- Explain how samsara can affect the lives of Buddhists.
- To what extent does samsara have a negative effect on Buddhist communities?
- How far do you agree that belief in samsara is not essential to Buddhism?

| Question Focus | The effect of the Three Poisons (Higher only) |
|---|---|

*You need to know:*
- what the Three Poisons are
- the role each one plays in the human condition
- why they are seen as poisons
- the effect they have on daily life
- the effect they have on the journey to nibbana
- where they fit into Buddhism as a whole.

*You need to avoid:*
- spending too much time giving descriptions of the pig, the cockerel and the snake – concentrate on their effects.

*You need to look out for:*
- questions that focus on one of the poisons and ask you to discuss it
- questions that suggest the problems of the poisons are not as great as they seem.

**Question approaches**

*Statements:*
- 'Hatred is the Root Poison that is the biggest obstacle to achieving nibbana.'
- 'Ignorance is what keeps Buddhists rooted in this reality.'
- 'The Three Root Poisons are at the heart of human suffering.'
- 'The Three Root Poisons are just human nature. There is not a problem with them.'

*Questions:*
- Using examples, show how moha affects the lives of Buddhists.
- Explain what benefits Buddhist society might feel if dosa is overcome.
- How important is the practice of non attachment in tackling the Three Root Poisons?
- Can the effects of the Three Root Poisons be controlled?
- Why do individuals find it very difficult to control the Three Root Poisons?

# THE GOALS OF LIFE

| Question Focus | Benefits and difficulties and importance of kamma |
|---|---|

*You need to know:*
- what kamma is
- the ways in which kamma can benefit and create difficulties for individuals and communities
- where kamma fits into Buddhism as a whole.

*You need to avoid:*
- simply repeating the law of kamma – it's very easy to fall into this trap.

*You need to look out for:*
- questions that focus on one of the benefits or problems and ask you to discuss it.

**Question approaches**

*Statements:*
- 'Kamma puts everyone in charge of their own destiny.'
- 'Kamma can benefit both the individual and the community.'
- 'Practising kamma is pointless because there is no soul.'
- 'Belief in kamma is worthwhile only if the individual survives death.'
- 'Kamma makes no difference to the lives of ordinary Buddhists.'

*Questions:*
- How can kamma work if Buddhists believe in anatta?
- Explain the two benefits of believing in kamma.
- Explain how kamma can affect the lives of Buddhists.
- To what extent does kamma have a negative effect on Buddhist communities?
- How far do you agree that belief in kamma is not essential to Buddhism?

> **Question Focus**    Issues related to the Buddhist goals of life

*You need to know:*
- that the most common issue referred to is the goals of Buddhism being selfish – so be ready for this one!
- what the goals of life are
- which aspects of each goal seem to be centred on the individual/good of the community
- which goal seems to be the most accessible
- which goals are the most difficult and the most beneficial.

*You need to avoid:*
- taking one side or the other (if the question permits) – it's far better to take a middle line.

*You need to look out for:*
- questions that focus on one of the goals.

**Question approaches**

*Statements:*
- 'Since nobody can describe what nibbana is, it is hardly a goal worth pursuing.'
- 'The Buddhist goals of life are concerned only about individual spiritual progress.'

- 'There is nothing in nibbana that will benefit the Buddhist community as a whole.'
- 'In Buddhism, pursuing the goals of life is essentially a selfish activity.'
- 'Nibbana is so remote a goal that for most Buddhists it is impossible to achieve it.'
- 'The best a Buddhist can aim for is good kamma.'
- 'Skilful actions are the most practical and beneficial of all the goals of Buddhism.'

*Questions:*
- Why is nibbana considered to be the hardest goal to achieve?
- Is there anything in the Buddhist goals of life that might benefit the community rather than the individual?
- Why do some Buddhists consider achieving nibbana too difficult for the laity?
- To what extent is achieving nibbana something that is only for the monastic community?
- Do you consider the Buddhist goals of life to be selfish?
- Why are skilful actions and kamma often considered the most realistic goals for the laity?

| Question Focus | Importance, benefits, problems and role of skilful and unskilful actions (Higher only) |
|---|---|

*You need to know:*
- what skilful and unskilful actions are and their importance
- their place in the life of lay Buddhists and monastic Buddhism
- their role in attaining nibbana
- benefits and problems arising from skilful and unskilful actions for individuals and for the community.

*You need to avoid:*
- confusing skilful and unskilful actions with kamma (although they can be a part of it).

*You need to look out for:*
- questions that focus on either skilful or unskilful actions
- questions that ask you to discuss how such actions help or hinder an individual's quest for nibbana
- questions that ask whether it is easier for monks, nuns or laity to perform skilful actions.

**Question approaches**

*Statements:*
- 'Only when skilful actions are practised can the individual attain nibbana.'
- 'It is understanding what nibbana is that helps Buddhists to achieve it; not practising skilful actions.'
- 'Unskilful actions are the main barrier to nibbana.'
- 'Buddhist monasteries are the only places where skilful actions have a chance of being successfully practised.'
- 'Lay Buddhists have no chance of getting rid of unskilful actions.'
- 'Skilful actions are designed only for monks to practise – they are beyond most lay people.'

*Questions:*
- To what extent do skilful actions benefit the sangha?
- How far do you agree that skilful actions are essential if Buddhists are to achieve nibbana?
- Explain the main moral principles behind skilful and unskilful actions.
- How damaging can unskilful actions be to individual Buddhists?
- Explain the ways in which skilful and unskilful actions are related to kamma.

| Question Focus | Nibbana understandings, comparisons and issues |
|---|---|

*You need to know:*
- different understandings of what nibbana is and how it is attained
- who is thought to be best placed to achieve it
- the extent to which it could be seen as selfish
- the benefits and drawbacks of achieving nibbana
- the extent to which it is a difficult goal to achieve
- differences in views between different Buddhist traditions.

*You need to avoid:*
- confusing Mahayana and Theravada understandings of nibbana
- describing too much in a comparison – compare, don't just describe.

*You need to look out for:*
- questions that focus on Mahayana or Theravada understanding of nibbana.

**Question approaches**

*Statements:*
- 'A goal that can only be experienced and cannot be described is hardly a goal worth aiming for.'
- 'Only monks can attain nibbana.'
- 'Because nibbana can only be experienced there is no chance of agreement on what it actually is.'
- 'Attaining nibbana is essentially a selfish pursuit.'
- 'It is necessary that nibbana can be attained by only a few.'
- 'Nibbana involves the destruction of the ego so it is really not a very attractive goal at all.'
- 'Therevada Buddhism's view of who achieves nibbana shows that its only concern is monks.'
- 'The Buddha would have preferred the Mahayanist view of nibbana.'

*Questions:*
- Why do Mahayanists and Theravadins have different views on nibbana?
- Explain the main differences between Mahayanist and Therevadin views of nibbana.
- How far do you agree that nibbana is possible only for monks?
- Explain two drawbacks of believing that only monks can attain nibbana.
- Why, according to Mahayana Buddhism, is achieving nibbana possible for lay people?
- Why is achieving nibbana considered to be so difficult?
- Why is being morally good an essential part of achieving nibbana?

# MEANS TO THE GOALS

 **Question Focus**    **Issues relating to the sangha (Higher only)**

*You need to know:*
- that the sangha is both the lay community and the monastic community
- benefits and drawbacks of monastic life and of practising faith in lay life
- impact of the sangha on the Buddhist community
- the importance of the sangha
- impact of monks and nuns on Buddhist life
- importance of the role of monks and nuns on Buddhist communities.

*You need to avoid:*

- confusing different understandings of the sangha
- forgetting what words such as 'lay', 'monastic', 'clergy', 'laity' and 'ascetic' mean
- relying too much on description – in this topic that is very easy to do
- taking sides where a choice is given – try to take the middle line because it will give you more to say.

*You need to look out for:*

- questions that relate the sangha to the goals of life.

**Question approaches**

*Statements:*

- 'The most important aspect of the sangha is its moral influence on lay people and monks.'
- 'The role of the sangha is more than just helping people to achieve nibbana.'
- 'Of the Three Jewels, the sangha is the most important.'
- 'The true sangha is the monastic sangha.'
- 'The monastic sangha is one of the extremes that the Buddha rejected.'
- 'The sangha is at the heart of Buddhism.'
- 'Monks and nuns are essential to the survival of the sangha as a whole.'

*Questions:*

- Why is the sangha so important in Buddhism?
- Why is the sangha considered to be more than just the monastic sangha?
- How important is the sangha in the individual's quest to achieve nibbana?
- To what extent does the sangha influence the moral conduct of Buddhists?
- How significant is the sangha in the individual's quest for nibbana?
- Explain two benefits of the sangha for Buddhists.

| Question Focus | Importance, benefits and difficulties of meditation |
|---|---|

*You need to know:*

- what the different types of meditation are (both in English and in the Buddhist terms) and how it is done
- importance of meditation for lay and monastic Buddhists

- benefits and drawbacks of meditation for the laity and the community
- benefits and drawbacks of meditation for monks
- the differences between the types of meditation
- the role of moral behaviour in meditation.

*You need to avoid:*
- confusing different types of meditation
- spending ages describing meditation in an AE question
- relying too much on description – in this topic that is very easy to do
- meditating during the exam; time is short.

*You need to look out for:*
- questions that pick out a type of meditation
- opportunities to give examples from real life.

**Question approaches**

*Statements:*
- 'Meditation can properly be practised only by monks.'
- 'Good moral behaviour is more important than meditation.'
- 'Meditation allows individuals to see the world for what it is.'
- 'Vipassana meditation is less beneficial to the individual than samatha meditation.'
- 'Without vipassana meditation there is no point to samatha meditation.'
- 'Meditation is so inward looking that it cannot possibly bring benefits to the community.'
- 'The main drawback of Buddhist meditation techniques is that nobody seems to benefit from them other than the person meditating.'

*Questions:*
- Why is meditation such an attractive activity?
- How important is meditation in Buddhism?
- Explain two drawbacks of meditation.
- To what extent does meditation benefit the community?
- Explain the differences between vipassana and samatha meditation.
- How important is the role of morality in meditation?
- What are the differences between Therevada and Mahayana Buddhism in their approach to meditation?
- To what extent is meditation the most important method of achieving nibbana?

| Question Focus | Benefits and difficulties of the Eightfold Path |
|---|---|

*You need to know:*
- the Eightfold Path (at least the bits you are meant to know)
- the importance of the Eightfold Path for lay and monastic Buddhists
- benefits and drawbacks of the Eightfold Path for the laity and the community
- benefits and drawbacks of the Eightfold Path for monks
- the role of morality in the Eightfold Path
- how the Eightfold Path helps people achieve nibbana.

*You need to avoid:*
- describing all the steps of the Eightfold Path
- confusing the steps of the Eightfold Path.

*You need to look out for:*
- questions that pick out one step of the Eightfold Path
- questions that identify themes in the Eightfold Path, such as morality.

**Question approaches**

*Statements:*
- 'The Eightfold Path brings many benefits to the Buddhist community.'
- 'The Eightfold Path can hardly be described as the middle way since many of the steps are very demanding.'
- 'The Threefold Way is beyond most ordinary Buddhists.'
- 'What makes the Eightfold Path of value to the whole community are its moral principles.'
- 'Only monks can truly hope to follow the Eightfold Path.'
- 'Following the Eightfold Path is the most important action lay Buddhists can take on their journey to nibbana.'

*Questions:*
- Why is right speech such an important step?
- Why might right livelihood be a major challenge today?
- How practical is the Eightfold Path in the twenty-first century?
- Why are the moral principles of the Eightfold Path so important?
- Explain two ways in which the Eightfold Path can bring benefits to individual Buddhists.

- Making three points, explain why the Eightfold Path might be a problem for some people in the Buddhist community?

---

| Question Focus | Importance and role of worship |
| --- | --- |

*You need to know:*

- different forms of worship in which Buddhists participate
- the purpose and role of worship in Buddhism (in the community and in the monastery)
- benefits, drawbacks and importance of worship.

*You need to avoid:*

- in an AE question, describing how Buddhists worship; focus on the why information.

*You need to look out for:*

- questions that focus on one aspect of worship.

**Question approaches**

*Statements:*

- 'Meditation is more important than worship.'
- 'Some people claim that Buddhists do not worship God, so worship is therefore pointless.'
- 'Worship brings the Buddhist community together.'
- 'Worship just confuses matters for Buddhists because in the strictest sense Buddha is not a God.'

*Questions:*

- Explain the significance of worship in two Buddhist traditions.
- Why do Buddhists worship?
- Why might some Buddhists see worship as a pointless exercise?
- How important is worship in Buddhism?

---

| Question Focus | Importance, benefits and difficulties of the Five Precepts |
| --- | --- |

*You need to know:*

- what the Five Precepts are
- what impact they have on Buddhists lives, laity, monks and nuns
- the themes of the precepts
- benefits and difficulties of the Five Precepts.

*You need to avoid:*
- describing all precepts and not analysing them
- confusing the precepts with the Eightfold Path.

*You need to look out for:*
- questions that pick out one of the precepts
- questions that identify themes in the precepts, such as non harm.

**Question approaches**

*Statements:*
- 'The Five Precepts benefit both the individual and the community.'
- 'The Five Precepts are no longer relevant.'
- 'The Five Precepts are easier for monks to follow than for the laity.'
- 'The Five Precepts are basically about respect for other people.'

*Questions:*
- Explain one benefit of the Five Precepts.
- Of the Five Precepts, which one do Buddhists consider to be the most challenging?
- Why do Buddhists follow the Five Precepts?
- To what extent are the Five Precepts easier for monks to follow?
- Why might abstaining from killing prove to be difficult for Buddhists to obey?
- Are the Five Precepts relevant in today's world?

| **Question Focus** | **Importance, benefits and difficulties of being a monk or nun (Higher only)** |
| --- | --- |

*You need to know:*
- the lifestyle of monks and nuns
- the importance and impact of monks and nuns in Buddhism
- benefits and drawbacks of living as a monk or nun
- whether it is easier to attain nibbana as a monk or lay person
- why monastic life is the preference of some Buddhists.

*You need to avoid:*
- giving too stereotypical a view of monks and nuns
- being too one-sided – try to be balanced if the question permits.

*You need to look out for:*
- questions that focus on one particular role of monks and nuns
- questions that focus on one tradition.

**Question approaches**

*Statements:*
- 'The importance of bhikkus to Buddhism can never be underestimated.'
- 'The life of a bhikku is both challenging and difficult.'
- 'The monastic community in Buddhism bring many benefits to the lay community.'
- 'Living in a monastery means that most Buddhist monks are out of touch with real life'
- 'The ideal Buddhist is one who lives the monastic life.'

*Questions:*
- Why are bhikkus so important in Buddhism?
- Explain two difficulties associated with living as a monk.
- Explain the differences between the Mahayanist and Therevadin views of monks.
- Why do some people consider monks to be the ideal Buddhists?
- Explain three benefits monks and nuns bring to Buddhist communities.
- How far do you agree that Buddhism could not survive without monks and nuns?
- To what extent are monks and nuns essential to Buddhism?

> **Question Focus**    **Importance, benefits, drawbacks and comparison of arhat and bodhisattva**

*You need to know:*
- what an arhat and bodhisattva are
- the roles of and reasons for the two in different traditions
- the impact of both on their respective communities
- why arhats may be considered self-centred individuals
- why bodhisattvas may be considered compassionate individuals
- importance of bodhisattvas and arhats.

*You need to avoid:*
- confusing bodhisattva with arhat
- confusing which one belongs to which tradition
- being too one-sided – where there is the opportunity, try to be balanced if the question permits.

*You need to look out for:*
- questions that focus on either the bodhisattva or the arhat
- questions that ask about the arhat or bodhisattva without mentioning their names
- questions that focus on one tradition.

**Question approaches**

*Statements:*
- 'Bodhisattvas are what the Buddha envisaged, not arhats.'
- 'The arhat is the perfect role model for all Buddhists.'
- 'Arhats have only one interest – themselves.'
- 'Bodhisattvas are the perfect role models for Buddhists.'
- 'The easiest way to achieve nibbana is to become an arhat.'

*Questions:*
- How important is compassion for a bodhisattva?
- To what extent do arhats represent the ideal Buddhist?
- How far do you agree with the view that arhats offer little to the Buddhist community?
- Explain three drawbacks of being an arhat.
- Explain the differences between two Buddhist traditions in their understanding of enlightened beings.
- Why do bodhisattvas remain on earth to help others attain enlightenment?

| **Question Focus** | **Importance, role and issues relating to the Dhamma** |
| --- | --- |

*You need to know:*
- content, role and importance of the Dhamma
- how the Dhamma helps Buddhists achieve the goals of life
- the role of the Dhamma in two different traditions.

*You need to avoid:*
- writing about one aspect of the Dhamma when the question requires more.

*You need to look out for:*
- questions that focus on the Dhamma in one tradition.

**Question approaches**

*Statements:*
- 'The Dhamma is the most important of the Three Jewels.'
- 'The Dhamma is even more important than the Buddha.'
- 'Without the Dhamma, enlightenment is impossible.'
- 'The teachings of the Dhamma have a positive effect on society as a whole.'
- 'In spite of its claims not to, the Dhamma teaches detachment from the world.'

*Questions:*
- Assess the importance of the Dhamma in Buddhism.
- Why is the Dhamma considered to be essential to attaining nibbana?
- How far do you agree that the Dhamma is as relevant today as it was when it was originally compiled?
- Explain the status of the Dhamma in two Buddhist traditions you have studied.

| Question Focus | Importance, role and issues relating to the life and teachings of the Buddha |
|---|---|

*You need to know:*
- the main events, role and importance of the Buddha's life
- how the Buddha helps Buddhists achieve the goals of life
- the role of the Buddha in two different traditions.

*You need to avoid:*
- writing about the life story of the Buddha when you are not asked to.

*You need to look out for:*
- questions that focus on the Buddha in one tradition.

**Question approaches**

*Statements:*
- 'It does not matter if the story of the Buddha is mainly a myth.'
- 'The life of the Buddha is symbolic of the struggle everyone has to come to terms with reality.'
- 'The main themes of Buddha's teaching are self-discipline and compassion for others.'
- 'Nobody can truly live up to the ideals of the Buddha.'
- 'In Therevada Buddhism, the Buddha is not as important as the Dhamma.'

*Questions:*

- How far do you agree that the Buddha is an impossible role model to follow?
- How important were the Four Sights in the life of the Buddha?
- What made Buddha come to the conclusion that the Middle Way was how to gain enlightenment?
- Why did the Buddha establish the Sangha?
- Why are there different views on the nature of the Buddha within Buddhism?

# 13    World religions – Christianity

*The human condition*

*The goals of life*

*Means to the goals*

## THE HUMAN CONDITION

> **Question Focus**    **Christian view of the human condition, pessimistic or realistic**

*You need to know:*
- the various aspects of the human condition
- the general characteristics of the human condition, e.g. suffering, death, alienation
- which aspects of the human condition are negative/positive/realistic
- how Christian views compare with actual experience.

*You need to avoid:*
- taking one side – try to be balanced when the question permits.

*You need to look out for:*
- any words in questions on this theme that could mean positive, negative, realistic, unrealistic – you use the same information
- the expression 'human condition' – you must know what it means
- questions that focus on one aspect of the human condition
- questions being phrased as 'How accurate are ...?'

**Question approaches**

*Statements:*
- 'Christian views of the human condition are very pessimistic.'

- 'Christian views of the human condition give an accurate description of it.'
- 'Life is not as bad as Christian understandings make it out to be.'
- 'There is little evidence that the Christian view of the human condition is either fair or accurate.'
- 'Christian views of life devalue its meaning and importance.'
- 'Christians say that human existence is characterised by sin; nothing can be further from the truth.'

*Questions:*
- To what extent are Christian views of the human condition negative?
- Why might some people view Christian teaching on human disobedience as a negative teaching?
- How important is belief in the Fall in understanding the human condition?
- Why is sin considered to be an important aspect of Christian beliefs about the human condition?
- Why is the Christian view of the human condition considered to be realistic?

| Question Focus | Positive or negative effects of the human condition on Christians |
|---|---|

*You need to know:*
- the various aspects of the human condition
- the general characteristics of the human condition, e.g. suffering, death, free will and alienation
- which aspects of the human condition have a good/bad effect on people
- what problems the different aspects of the human condition can cause people.

*You need to avoid:*
- seeing the Christian view of human life as being entirely negative.

*You need to look out for:*
- questions that refer to how Christians feel about the human condition
- the expression 'human condition' – you must know what it means
- questions that focus on one aspect of the human condition.

**Question approaches**

*Statements:*
- 'Christian teachings on the nature of human beings offer hope.'

- 'Sin is so inescapable that it is enough to make a person want to give up trying.'
- 'Christian teaching on alienation has a positive effect on Christians.'
- 'There are no positives that can be taken out of the belief that humans are alienated from God, nature and each other.'
- 'Free will is what gives Christians hope of overcoming the human condition.'
- 'God gives Christians hope of overcoming the human condition.'
- 'Freewill has more negatives than pluses.'

*Questions:*

- Why is belief in free will a positive belief for many Christians?
- How important is original sin in the human condition?
- Why might Christians disagree that their view of the human condition is negative?
- To what extent does Christian belief in sin affect their lives?
- Do you agree that the greatest challenge of the human condition is using free will responsibly?

| Question Focus | Centrality of individual concepts to the human condition (including the relationship between different concepts and different aspects being the key to understanding it) |
|---|---|

*You need to know:*

- the various aspects of the human condition
- the general characteristics of the human condition, e.g. suffering, death, free will and alienation
- how the different aspects of the human condition are related to each other
- how they can all be central in some way.

*You need to avoid:*

- missing out one of the aspects in your discussion of centrality
- disagreeing with centrality questions if you can avoid it – the best thing is to argue is that none is more central than the other, and go on to show how they are interrelated

- giving a description of the human condition without mentioning centrality – it will get you no marks
- your teacher, if you do a religion other than the one you have studied!

*You need to look out for:*

- the different ways in which centrality-type questions can be asked
- the expression 'human condition' – you must know what it means

- questions that focus on one aspect of the human condition and ask about its centrality
- questions that ask you to discuss two or more related aspects of the human condition.

## Question approaches

*Statements:*
- 'Original sin is central to Christian understandings of the human condition.'
- 'Free will is at the heart of Christian teachings on the human condition.'
- 'Understanding free will is more important than understanding any other part of the human condition.'
- 'If Christians do not accept that humans are responsible for sin, they have no chance of understanding the human condition.'
- 'Adam and Eve are the root cause of alienation.'
- 'The beauty of Christian understandings of the human condition is the way all the concepts are connected to each other.'
- 'Original sin is not the fault of humans; it is the fault of the God that gave them it.'
- 'Free will is the sole cause of sin.'

*Questions:*
- To what extent is alienation central to the human condition?
- For Christians, what is the key aspect of the human condition?
- How far do you agree that disobedience is central to Christian understandings of the human condition?
- How successfully can it be argued that the Fall is at the heart of Christian understandings of the human condition?
- Why is original sin such an important aspect of the human condition?
- To what extent is free will the cause of human suffering?

| Question Focus | Different aspects of the human condition as the key problem in the human condition |
|---|---|

*You need to know:*
- the various aspects of the human condition
- the problems that each individual aspect can cause
- which ones seem to cause the most and the fewest problems
- the importance of understanding each one in relation to achieving eternal life

- the effects of each one in relation to creating problems in relationships with God.

*You need to avoid:*
- straying off course – it's very easy to do this and end up talking about the goals instead of the human condition.

*You need to look out for:*
- the different ways in which questions about issues arising from each aspect are asked
- the expression 'human condition' – you must know what it means
- questions that focus on one aspect of the human condition and ask about its problems
- questions that ask you to discuss two or more related aspects of the human condition.

## Question approaches

*Statements:*
- 'Human disobedience is the key problem of the human condition.'
- 'Abuse of free will is at the heart of Christian understandings of the human condition.'
- 'It's alienation from God that must be overcome.'
- 'Suffering and death are not the result of the Fall.'

*Questions:*
- Why is alienation from God a key issue in Christian teachings about the human condition?
- To what extent is control of free will the main problem of the human condition?
- Explain the difficulties Christians might have in explaining the origins of sin.
- Why is fixing human relationships with God so important to Christians?

| Question Focus | Benefits and difficulties of overcoming the human condition |
|---|---|

*You need to know:*
- the various aspects of the human condition
- the benefits and difficulties of each one
- the ways in which each one can be overcome (means to the goals)

- how overcoming the problems can help individuals
- the difficulties and benefits of overcoming the human condition.

*You need to avoid:*
- writing about the centrality of different aspects of the human condition – this question is not about that
- getting different aspects of the human condition mixed up.

*You need to look out for:*
- questions that focus on one or two aspects of the human condition and ask you to discuss them in relation to benefits and difficulties
- questions that look for some kind of comparison of the benefits and difficulties
- questions that state a benefit or difficulty and ask you to explain it.

**Question approaches**

*Statements:*
- 'Once Christians understand the human condition, their suffering ends.'
- 'The main benefits of overcoming the human condition are seen more in the individual rather than the community.'
- 'The problem with overcoming the human condition is that it involves a pessimistic view of the world.'
- 'Destroying the effects of sin is the main benefit from understanding the human condition.'

*Questions:*
- Explain the main benefits for Christians of overcoming the human condition.
- Why might it be argued that there is nothing attractive about overcoming the human condition?
- Explain the difficulties Christians might have in explaining suffering.
- Why might understanding suffering bring benefits to Christians?

| Question Focus | Implications of free will |
| --- | --- |

*You need to know:*
- the role of free will in the origin of sin
- the relationship between free will and sin
- the problems caused by free will
- different understandings of free will
- implications of free will for the nature of God/for Christians.

*You need to avoid:*
- confusing the very different Christian views of free will
- using your free will to dodge RMPS revision on a Thursday night after school
- telling your parents that there is no such thing as free will, so that your act of coming in at 2 a.m. was predestined by powers greater than yourself.

*You need to look out for:*
- questions that focus on linking free will to sin or disobedience
- questions that suggest free will is the key to understanding the human condition.

**Question approaches**

*Statements:*
- 'Free will has been the downfall of humans.'
- 'The gift of free will is the greatest gift that God has given us.'
- 'Since God gave us the gift of free will we cannot be held accountable for abusing it.'
- 'Everything is a free choice; God has predestined nothing.'

*Questions:*
- Why is free will considered to be a gift from God?
- Do Christians agree on their understanding of free will?
- Why might some people feel that the blame for the Fall should be shared between God and humans?
- To what extent is human free will responsible for human alienation from nature and fellow humans?
- Why did God permit humans to have free will?

| Question Focus | Impact of stewardship on the lives of Christians (Higher only) |
| --- | --- |

*You need to know:*
- what stewardship means
- the role stewardship plays in the human condition
- the effect it has on daily life
- where it fits into Christianity as a whole.

*You need to avoid:*
- confusing it with stewarding the Earth's resources.

*You need to look out for:*
- questions that focus on this small area – missing this area from your revision could be an expensive mistake!

## Question approaches

*Statements:*
- 'Stewardship begins and ends with believing that God owns our lives.'
- 'Christians have a God-given duty to improve his creation.'
- 'There is more to being a Christian than repentance.'
- 'Stewardship brings great benefits not just to Christians but to the community as a whole.'
- 'Christian stewardship has changed the world.'

*Questions:*
- Why might some people object to Christian stewardship of the world?
- To what extent is Christian stewardship effective in the modern world?
- Why might Christians feel that repentance is not enough to be a Christian?
- Explain three effects of Christian stewardship on the world.

> **Question Focus**  **Issues related to the story of the Fall**

*You need to know:*
- the story, interpretation and implications of the Fall
- the implications of the story for God
- the place of the story in Christian belief.

*You need to avoid:*
- telling the whole creation story if the question is about the Fall.

*You need to look out for:*
- questions that ask about how Christians explain the origin of sin – the Fall is just one way that they explain it, not the only way.

## Question approaches

*Statements:*
- 'The story of the Fall is symbolic, not historical.'
- 'God can, in no way, be held responsible for original sin.'
- 'The Fall of humanity is an historical event.'

- 'The meaning of the story of Adam and Eve is more important than the story itself.'
- 'The Genesis account of original sin is fundamental to Christian belief.'

*Questions:*

- How far do you agree that it is not necessary to treat the story of the Fall as an historical event?
- Evaluate the claim that belief in original sin is essential to Christian belief.
- Explain two issues associated with the Genesis story of Adam and Eve's sin.
- Why do some Christians consider it better to view the story of the Fall as symbolic rather than literal truth?
- Aside from the story of the Fall, in what other ways might Christians explain the existence of sin and evil in the world?

# THE GOALS OF LIFE

| Question Focus | Importance, relevance, benefits and difficulties of following Jesus' example and teachings |
| --- | --- |

*You need to know:*

- examples of Jesus' teachings and actions
- the ways in which Jesus' teachings can benefit and create difficulties for individuals and the community
- the ways in which Jesus' example can benefit and create difficulties for individuals and the community
- the impact of Jesus' teachings on Christianity as a whole
- individual difficulties and benefits that may be the focus of a question
- the relevance, importance and application of Jesus' teachings today
- how Jesus' teachings and example can lead people to salvation.

*You need to avoid:*

- simply listing his teachings
- saying that his example is impossible to follow – it's too difficult to back that up.

*You need to look out for:*

- questions that focus on one of the benefits or problems and ask you to discuss it
- questions that ask you about the relevance of Jesus' teachings today.

**Question approaches**

*Statements:*
- 'Jesus' teachings are not practical in Scotland in the twenty-first century.'
- 'Following the teachings of Jesus today helps to make individuals more compassionate.'
- 'Jesus' teachings are fine in theory, but, in practice, most of them are impossible.'
- 'Jesus' teachings tell us more about how to behave than what God is like.'
- 'Jesus' teachings and actions are designed to benefit the community more than the individual.'

*Questions:*
- To what extent are the teachings of Jesus relevant today?
- Explain how Christians overcome the challenges of following Jesus' example in the twenty-first century.
- Using two examples, explain how a teaching of Jesus can be applied today.
- How far do you agree that living a life according to Christian teachings improves the quality of an individual's life?

**Question Focus** — **The role of Jesus in salvation**

*You need to know:*
- what Jesus' role in salvation is
- the effect of Jesus on human relationships with God
- whether, or not, belief in Jesus is essential to salvation
- the impact, meaning and purpose of Jesus' life in general and on Christians
- why Jesus was necessary
- the different interpretations of the importance of Jesus.

*You need to avoid:*
- simply describing what Christians believe about Jesus.

*You need to look out for:*
- questions that focus on how essential belief in Jesus is to gaining salvation.

**Question approaches**

*Statements:*
- 'Without Jesus, salvation is impossible.'
- 'Only through Jesus can humanity's relationship with God be restored.'

- 'Jesus is the one and only way back to God.'
- 'Jesus' death was necessary.'
- 'Jesus changes lives.'
- 'Jesus is alive.'

*Questions:*
- How far do Christians agree that Jesus is the sole means to salvation for all humanity?
- To what extent does belief in Jesus change the lives of individuals?
- Why do Christians consider Jesus' death to be necessary?
- Explain the relationship between Jesus and the Fall.

> **Question Focus**    **Issues related to the Christian goals of life plus the easiest, hardest, realistic and most relevant goal of life to achieve**

*You need to know:*
- what the goals of life are
- which aspects of each goal seem to be centred on the individual
- which aspects of each goal seem to be centred on the good of the community
- which goal seems to be the most accessible, most difficult or most beneficial.

*You need to avoid:*
- taking one side or the other (if the question permits) – it's far better to take a middle line.

*You need to look out for:*
- questions that focus on one of the goals.

**Question approaches**

*Statements:*
- 'Developing a relationship with God through prayer is a far more realistic goal than trying to follow the example of Jesus.'
- 'Christian goals of life benefit the individual more than the community.'
- 'The main theme of Christian goals of life is to love your neighbour.'
- 'For Christians, the main goal of life is avoiding hell.'
- 'Living the Christian life is the most important goal in Christian life.'

*Questions:*
- Why do Christians see judgement as a goal of life?

- Explain the benefits that may arise for Christians from developing a relationship with God.
- Why is there such an emphasis on following Jesus' example?
- For Christians, is following Jesus' example more important as a goal of life than gaining eternal life?
- How far do Christians agree that there is no place for belief in hell in Christianity?

| Question Focus | Benefits and difficulties of various aspects of worship |
|---|---|

*You need to know:*
- how Christians worship
- different aspects of worship
- the types and role of prayer
- the effectiveness of prayer
- views and uses of prayer.

*You need to avoid:*
- thinking that prayer is only petitionary
- that prayer is the only aspect of worship.

*You need to look out for:*
- questions that focus on aspects of worship other than prayer.

**Question approaches**

*Statements:*
- 'Prayer is at the heart of spiritual development.'
- 'Christians can grow spiritually only if there is communal worship.'
- 'Prayer achieves very little.'
- 'Personal private worship is more meaningful than communal worship.'

*Questions:*
- To what extent is the Bible central to Christian worship?
- Explain two benefits Christians may receive from worship.
- How far do you agree that traditional Christianity is no longer relevant?
- Why do some Christians believe that all prayers are answered?
- Has Christian worship got any meaningful purpose left today?

# MEANS TO THE GOALS

| Question Focus | Issues, benefits, difficulties, interpretations and importance of the death and resurrection of Jesus |
|---|---|

*You need to know:*
- the story of the death and resurrection of Jesus
- how it relates to other concepts in the course
- its importance and impact on Christian life
- the importance of Jesus' suffering, death and resurrection
- how the suffering of Jesus is marked in Christian life and worship.

*You need to avoid:*
- confusing different understandings of the Passion
- forgetting what words like Passion and resurrection mean
- relying too much on description – that is very easy to do in this topic
- taking sides where a choice is given – try to take a middle line because it will give you more to say.

*You need to look out for:*
- questions that relate the Passion to the goals of life and human condition.

**Question approaches**

*Statements:*
- 'The Passion of Christ is central to Christian belief.'
- 'There is no doubt that Jesus' resurrection was physical.'
- 'Believing that Jesus' resurrection was physical is very problematic.'
- 'The resurrection gives Christians hope.'

*Questions:*
- Why do Christians consider Jesus' death to be important?
- To what extent is Jesus' resurrection more important than his death?
- How far do you agree with the view that belief in a physical resurrection is essential?
- Explain the differences between two understandings of Jesus' resurrection.
- Explain some of the problems associated with the resurrection of Jesus.
- Why do Christians view the resurrection as an essential part of their faith?
- Develop an argument that highlights the importance of Jesus' death.

> **Question Focus** | **Importance, benefits and difficulties of the sacraments (Higher only)**

*You need to know:*
- what a sacrament is
- how baptism and communion are done
- benefits and drawbacks of different types of baptism or communion
- the differences between each type of baptism or communion
- views on the differences
- the importance of baptism or communion
- where sacraments fit into the means to the goals
- what practical benefits either of them brings
- comparisons between sacraments and Christian action.

*You need to avoid:*
- confusing different types of sacraments
- forgetting the different words for the sacraments
- relying too much on description – that is very easy to do in this topic.

*You need to look out for:*
- questions that pick out one sacrament for comment
- questions that ask for a comparison of impacts of sacraments.

**Question approaches**

*Statements:*
- 'To be Christian, it is essential that individuals are baptised.'
- 'Adult baptism is more meaningful than infant baptism.'
- 'The Eucharist is central to all forms of Christian worship.'
- 'Ultimately, the sacraments are of no great importance in Christianity.'

*Questions:*
- Explain why some Christians prefer adult baptism to infant baptism.
- Why are there differences in the way Christians celebrate communion?
- How might Christians respond, if it was suggested that baptism is a meaningless and irrelevant ritual?
- Explain why some Christians consider baptism and communion to be essential to Christian life.

- How convincing are arguments in favour of adult baptism?
- How central are the sacraments to Christian life?

> **Question Focus**
>
> **Issues, benefits, drawbacks and importance of the Kingdom of God (specifically named at Higher, implied at Int 2)**

*You need to know:*
- what the Kingdom of God is
- how it fits into Christian life
- the reasons for its importance
- how it spreads
- its impact on Christians and the world.

*You need to avoid:*
- confusing it with action against social injustice, although that can be a part of the Kingdom of God
- relying too much on description – that is very easy to do in this topic
- taking sides where a choice is given – try to take a middle line, because it will give you more to say.

*You need to look out for:*
- questions that ask vaguely about the growth of the Kingdom of God in the world.

**Question approaches**

*Statements:*
- 'The Kingdom of God is fine in theory, but, in practice, it will never work.'
- 'The key ideas behind the kingdom of God are love God and love each other.'
- 'If everyone accepted the moral ideals of the Kingdom of God the world would be a better place.'
- 'The Kingdom of God allows the individual to develop spiritually and morally.'

*Questions:*
- Explain the reasons why some people might criticise the moral ideals of the Kingdom of God.
- Give an assessment of the weaknesses of belief in the Kingdom of God.
- What evidence would Christians use to support their view that the Kingdom of God makes a difference to the world?

- Why is participating in the Kingdom of God considered essential to Christian life?

- In your opinion, what concepts in the Kingdom of God are most likely to bring benefits to society?

- How can Christians make the Kingdom of God grow?

| **Question Focus** | **Issues, importance, benefits and difficulties of tackling social injustice** |
|---|---|

*You need to know:*
- what social injustice is

- what Christians say and do about it

- what Jesus did and taught about it

- why Christians are sometimes criticised for getting involved or not getting involved

- whether Christians should concentrate on the spiritual and leave the social to the politicians

- benefits and drawbacks of tackling social injustice

- views on tackling social injustice.

*You need to avoid:*
- forgetting to cover this topic

- being too vague in this topic – give clear examples to support your views.

*You need to look out for:*
- questions that ask for different types of Christian social action

- questions that ask for how far Christian social action puts Jesus' teaching into practice.

**Question approaches**

*Statements:*
- 'Christians should concentrate on God and not on social justice.'

- 'Christian action is far more important than Christian worship.'

- 'Being a Christian means you have to be involved in fighting for social justice.'

- 'To be relevant in the twenty-first century, Christians must tackle social injustice.'

- 'Just as Jesus tackled social injustice so too should modern-day Christians.'

*Questions:*

- Why should Christians become involved in tackling social injustice?
- To what extent is tackling social injustice a Christian duty?
- Explain three drawbacks of Christians becoming involved in the fight against social injustice.
- How important in the lives of Christians is tackling injustice?
- How far are Christians, who tackle social injustice, putting the teachings of Jesus into action?